MILLER'S

TEDDY Sue Pearson

BEARS

A Complete Collector's Guide

Miller's Teddy Bears: A Complete Collector's Guide
Sue Pearson

First published in Great Britain in 2001 by Miller's,
an imprint of Octopus Publishing Group Ltd,
2–4 Heron Quays, London, E14 4JP

Miller's is a registered trademark of Octopus Publishing Group Ltd

© 2001 Octopus Publishing Group Ltd

Reprinted 2002

Commissioning Editor Anna Sanderson

Executive Art Editor Rhonda Fisher

Project Editor Emily Anderson

Design SteersMcGillan Ltd

Editor Claire Musters

Proofreader Miranda Stonor

Indexer Hilary Bird

Production Angela Couchman, Catherine Lay

Jacket Photography Peter Anderson, Michael Pearson

The publishers will be grateful for any information that will assist them in
keeping future editions up to date. While every care has been taken in the
preparation of this book, neither the author nor the publisher can accept
any liability for any consequence arising from the use thereof, or the
information contained therein.

ISBN 1 84000 391 X

A CIP catalogue record for this book is available from the British Library

Set in Goudy Sans and Frutiger

Produced by Toppan Printing Co., (HK) Ltd.

Printed and bound in China

Front of jacket: selection of vintage bears of all kinds and by many different makers
Front flap: Steiff bear in red jumper, c.1908, £4,500–5,500 ($6,750–8,250)
Back flap: restored Steiff sailor bear with leather feet, c.1908 £3,500–4,500 ($5,250–6,750)
Back of jacket: group of bears including a Steiff RolyPoly valued at £4,000–6,000 ($6,000–9,000)

Title page: group of three bears – two 1930s Chilterns and one, c.1915, by an unknown American maker,
left to right: £500–600 ($750–900), £200–300 ($300–450), £300–400 ($450–600)

Contents page: Steiff teddy clown c.1925, Steiff ball and Steiff bear c.1908,
left to right: £6,000–7,000 ($9,000–10,500), £200–300 ($300–450), £4,000–5,000 ($6,000–7,500)

CONTENTS

FOREWORD

I have loved teddy bears ever since I was a child. My mother gave me our family's old bear to play with and that bear became my constant companion and friend. I still have him with me today.

When I first started collecting bears I just bought them purely on their looks alone – it was their faces that attracted me but I had no idea who the manufacturer was in each case or if they were valuable or not. In those days bears were much cheaper and easier to obtain. They could often be found sitting at the back of junk shops next to antique china dolls and toys, having been cleared out of old houses together with the furniture.

There were also not so many collectors around in the 1960s. However, in the 1970s and '80s the interest in collecting bears spread to England from the USA and with it came the emergence of a growing number of specialist doll and toy fairs. Americans, and Californians in particular, began to make artist bears and sell them at doll and teddy bear fairs in the USA and UK. This encouraged people to start collecting vintage bears as well, which coincided with old bears beginning to appear more often in auctions. Soon after this, I decided to turn my hobby into a business. I began by selling dolls and teddy bears at fairs and then set up a tiny stall in a Brighton market. Eventually I realized my true ambition and opened a shop in the Lanes in Brighton. People often ask me how I can part with the bears I have in my shop. Sometimes I can't and have to keep one that has caught my eye with his special appeal, whether he is valuable or not.

Bears can be frustrating at times because they don't always come with a label that identifies them. Occasionally I get a bear that is quite different from anything I have ever seen before. When that happens I really wish he could speak and tell me where he has come from…

Old teddy bears have long been children's toys and they have often been passed down through several generations of one particular family. Some older bears have even been through both world wars. They are always loyal, much-loved friends, which is often shown by their battered appearance. For me, this provides a wonderful sense of history and also gives them a very special charm.

I feel extremely privileged to be able to combine a hobby and a business that enables me to meet some wonderful people who all share a love of teddy bears. I get thousands of requests from people who want me to identify their own bears for them. This is especially the case now that the Internet has brought collectors from all over the world even closer. I hope, therefore, that this book will help you to find out the identity of your own favourite bear, and that you can experience with me the joy I have had from collecting teddy bears over the years.

Sue Pearson

VALENTINA
Valentina is one of Sue's favourite bears. She is a Strunz bear, c.1910, given to Sue by her husband as a surprise Valentine's Day present a few years ago. She is rather fragile and her dress and pinafore, made from a dress that belonged to her original owner, protects her from further deterioration. **Ht 53cm (21in), £550–650 ($825–975)**

CREATING A COLLECTION

A BRIEF HISTORY OF TEDDY BEARS

• 1904: the first Steiff bears with metal rods and elephant buttons were sold.

• 1905: Steiff produced a new design of bear, made with cardboard disc joints.

• 1920s: kapok stuffing was introduced.

• 1929: artificial silk plush was used for the first time, in a variety of colours.

• 1940–45: the design of teddy bears changed due to a shortage of materials; the new bears had shorter arms and legs, flatter faces and smaller humps.

• 1940–45: "sub" stuffing replaced kapok.

• 1950s: Wendy Boston made locked-in safety eyes and the first fully washable bear.

• 1950s and '60s: synthetic fabric and stuffing was used for the first time.

• 1959–60: plastic noses were used on Chiltern bears.

• 1960s and '70s: many unjointed bears were made, often in synthetic fabric.

• 1970s and '80s: the first artist bears were made in the USA and spread to the UK.

It is very important when creating a teddy bear collection to take things slowly. It can be tempting to rush out and buy in quantity, but bears should be acquired over the years – many wonderful collections have been created with time, patience and a lot of love. Some collections cost many thousands of pounds while others have been put together with much less money but give just as much pleasure. When starting a collection space can be a very important factor. If you are going to collect large bears, then you will need a large area to accommodate them; at the other end of the scale, miniature bears take up very little room. Another consideration is how extensive you want your collection to be: some collectors ration themselves to just a few bears a year, while others return from bear fairs with full bags. Your budget will be a deciding factor, but don't be disheartened if your limit is small – look out for later bears from the '60s and '70s or, if you like new bears, buy bears by budding artists as they are generally less expensive. Below are some general guidelines that will help when starting a collection.

TEDDY BEAR SHOPS
This picture shows the author, Sue Pearson, standing among her array of colourful vintage and artist teddy bears in her shop in the historic Lanes of Brighton. Sue also runs a teddy bear hospital, which admits many hundreds of patients each year.

LEARNING TO DATE BEARS

If you decide to collect vintage bears it is very important to become familiar with the various identifying features that will help you to recognize manufacturers and date the bear, as you may then pick up a bargain that someone else has missed. It is therefore a good idea to decide which type of bear interests you: some collectors choose English bears, others specialize in unjointed or coloured bears. Learning as much as possible about your chosen type will prove exciting and challenging.

You will need to have a general idea of how to date the bears that you see in order to find the right ones for your chosen area. Recognizing the important features of vintage bears can be quite difficult to begin with but, generally speaking, the longer the arms and nose then the older the bear. The earliest bears were modelled on real bears and stood on all fours – the early Steiff bears in particular have arms so long that they touch their feet. By contrast, English bears that were made after World War II, when mohair was hard to find, have short arms and flat faces due to the need to economize on fabric. Black button eyes were used on early bears but eyes have often been replaced, so just because a bear has button eyes does not mean it is definitely very old. You need to look at the features as a whole to build up a true picture. Look at the shape of the bear and ask: does he have a hump? what fabric is he made of? and what kind of stuffing does he have?

FEATURES THAT AID DATING

Wood wool, known as excelsior in the USA, is made up of fine wood shavings. This stuffing was used from the earliest times, but in the 1920s kapok was introduced – a natural, light, cotton-type of material that comes from the seedpod of a tree. Often a combination of the two is used in a bear – wood wool in the head and kapok in the body. If you gently squeeze a bear you can usually feel what type of stuffing has been used – wood wool crackles under gentle pressure, whereas kapok is soft to the touch. You may find a very old bear stuffed with cork or horsehair, while much later bears will be filled with synthetic stuffings. During and after World War II sub-stuffing, made from textile waste, was used instead of kapok, which was unavailable. From the 1950s foam chippings were adopted, and in the 1960s an all-in-one foam stuffing was introduced, manufactured under the name of Fairy Foam, which springs back into shape easily when pressed.

Most old bears have cardboard joints in order to allow them to move their head, arms and legs. The fabric most often used to make them was mohair plush, spun in the mills of Yorkshire and known as Yorkshire cloth. Many German makers imported this mohair from England and it has stood the test of time very well, as many old mohair bears have been handed down through generations of children and have still emerged intact, if a little battered. Mohair is still used on new bears made today. Art silk plush was introduced in 1930 and used on the many coloured bears that were so popular at the time. Synthetic fabrics were then developed and used after World War II.

Nose and claw stitching are very important aids to identification as each maker has their own distinctive design. Early Chiltern noses, for instance, have long upward end stitches, Merrythought bears have very unusual webbed claw stitching, and Chad Valley have long,

oblong, vertically stitched noses. It can be very difficult to identify an old bear that has lost its nose, claw stitching and eyes as these are the vital clues to their identity. It is extremely useful, therefore, to take time to learn more about the various styles. Eyes can be button, glass or plastic – the way to tell the difference is to press an eye against your cheek as the plastic will feel warm and the glass very cold. Plastic was introduced after World War II, but just because a bear has plastic eyes does not mean it was definitely made post-1945. They may be replacement eyes, put there for reasons of safety as many vintage bears had glass eyes on long metal wires, which parents considered dangerous. Paw pads can also tell you about the date of a bear: early bears have pads covered in felt or cotton; rexine and velvet were introduced at the end of the 1930s, but rexine was used principally in the 1950s and '60s.

Unfortunately you cannot rely on finding a label to identify the maker of a bear – too often there is just the mark to show where the label once was. When labels are present they are often found sewn on the foot pad or stitched into the side seam, but check carefully as they can turn up in the most unexpected places. Card labels, or tags, were used on many early bears, often attached to the chest by a horizontal stitch, but finding a bear with its original card label is a rarity.

These are just some of the things to look out for when trying to identify the age and maker of an old bear and further details are given throughout the book. It takes time to familiarize yourself with all the different characteristics, and some bears defy all attempts to identify them, but that does not matter as he will always be lovely in your eyes.

SOUGHT-AFTER STEIFF BEAR
This early 1908 centre-seam Steiff is in very good condition and has a most appealing face. Many collectors seek this type of bear but unfortunately they do not turn up very often, and when they do they command a high price.

CREATING A COLLECTION

NEW BEARS

When collecting teddy bears you do not have to focus on expensive antique examples. In the 1970s a completely different area of collecting emerged – new bears. These bears divide into two main categories that describe the people that make them – artists and manufacturers – and there is something to suit everyone's taste and pocket. Bear artist is the term used to describe a person who designs and makes his or her own bears. These artists are not manufacturers, as they produce small numbers of bears – often one-of-a-kinds or very limited editions. Manufacturers, on the other hand, produce thousands of copies of the same bear. Some of the very old companies, such as Steiff, Merrythought and Dean's, make newly manufactured bears and they have a large following for their limited editions, which they bring out each year. There are of course many new companies that are making bears too, such as Boyd's Bears, Robin Rive and many others, and their bears are widely available in gift shops around the world. Many of these new bears are made in the Far East.

WHERE TO FIND NEW BEARS

Many large stores such as Harrods and Hamleys in London sell their own limited-edition bears, as do the many specialist bear shops that can be found worldwide. It can be very interesting to visit teddy bear shops as they house a wide range of bears and the bear dealers are often very helpful and generous with their specialist knowledge. In a shop you will usually also have the opportunity to touch the various bears, which is important as every single bear has its own unique feel. Some new bears are hard stuffed while others are soft and squashy – you just need to decide what appeals to you before you decide which bear to buy.

ARTIST BEAR
This charming bear is made by Amy Goodrich of Portobello Bears. Amy is one of the top British bear artists and is well known worldwide. Her bears are made in the vintage style and are often dressed in antique clothing. These types of artist bears are very sought after by collectors.

BEARS AT
AUCTION
This Chiltern bear
from the 1930s would
be a "must have" if he
appeared in an auction. He
has an endearing expression
and is in excellent condition
but with luck he would not be
too expensive. He is wearing a
typical auction tag, with a
lot number on it to
identify him in the
catalogue.

TIPS FOR BUYING AT AUCTION

• Try and go to the viewing that takes place a few days before the sale and study the catalogue to familarize yourself with what is available.

• Before bidding you must register with the auction house by giving them your name and address.

• Decide on your limit before the auction sale starts and then stick to it. Remember that the final hammer price does not include the auction house premium, which is usually 10–20 per cent, or the tax on that premium.

The Internet has brought the buying and selling of bears straight into people's homes, which is great if you are unable to attend auctions in person or just want to learn about what is involved before taking part. Check the online auctions for specialist bears sales and visit the many dealer and shop websites to view their stock at leisure before buying. However, there is nothing to beat the excitement of a live auction. These can be specialist doll and toy auctions, of which bears will be a part, but it is also worth looking in a mixed sale of furniture and other household items. Boot fairs and flea markets are also a happy hunting ground for bargains, but you have to get up early to be lucky.

BUYING AT AUCTION

Despite some teddy bears fetching record-breaking prices at auction, and hitting the headlines as a result, some of the bears in these sales, even at the best-known auction houses such as Sotheby's, Christie's

VIEWING & BUYING BEARS

Visiting museums is a good way to see a variety of bears and there are many wonderful museums all over the world that feature both old and new bears, displayed in different settings (see pp.146–9); for example the Puppenhausmuseum in Basel has the most comprehensive collection of antique bears in the world. You can also see famous bears such as Teddy Girl, the most expensive bear ever sold at auction, who is now in a museum in Japan. Bears in museums are often displayed with other old toys and dolls of the same age to give a better sense of the period.

Teddy bear fairs are held worldwide (see pp.150–153) and these are wonderful places for a new collector to see and touch a huge selection of bears. There are usually specialist vintage bear dealers present who will be very helpful and talk you through their stock, especially if you tell them that you are new to collecting. Many teddy bear shops exhibit at these events and will show a range of their stock, including both old and new bears. A fair is also a good place to meet bear artists in person and look at their bears. You will be able to see their latest work and will soon learn to recognize their individual styles.

When buying old bears always get a proper receipt, stating the maker, if known, the approximate date and the name and address of the seller. This applies particularly when buying from general antiques shops or flea markets, especially if paying a substantial amount of money, and also from shops. You will need these receipts if you intend to insure your collection, for new as well as vintage bears.

NEW MANUFACTURED BEARS
This is an example of a new, limited-edition bear made by Steiff, sold only in the UK in the year 2000. He is a beautifully made bear with thick mohair, and a jolly Scottish tartan hat and scarf. Bears such as this are very popular with collectors and hold their value well.

CREATING A COLLECTION

and Phillips, can be bought at very reasonable prices. The smaller provincial salerooms will also provide a hunting ground for collectors. Going to an auction sale can seem a bit daunting to a new collector, but if you follow just a few simple guidelines it can prove to be a very rewarding and enjoyable experience. In order to be prepared for the bidding itself, it is advisable to go to the pre-sale viewing, where you will be able to examine the bears closely and ask the resident expert any questions you may have on a particular piece. The viewing normally occurs a day or two before the auction.

Once there take your time to examine closely any bears you are interested in. Check to see if the maker's label is still there – a Steiff bear may be missing its button but you should be able to tell that it had one originally as there may be a mark where it used to be. Condition is one of the most important factors when buying a bear, as it can affect the price dramatically. Bears in perfect condition are getting much harder to find so you must expect to pay considerably more if you are lucky enough to find one, although a very rare bear will always be expensive, whatever its condition. However, there is no need to pass on every bear that is not in pristine condition, and many collectors actually prefer well-loved bears. Thinning mohair, repairs and patches will affect the price, and coloured bears that have faded will be cheaper than bears with their original bright colours. Steiff Cinnamon bears are especially prone to ageing as the dye used weakened the mohair fabric. Watch out for fabric that is dry, brittle, and rotting as this is very difficult to restore as it crumbles away when sewing and restuffing is attemped. Missing fur is irreplaceable and the price paid should reflect condition. If you are in any doubt, you can request a free condition report on an individual lot.

Some bears are sold in a group as one lot; these tend to be the damaged or cheaper bears and often include old stuffed animals or even a golly. They are usually lumped together in a cardboard box,

WELL-LOVED BEAR
This magnificent Steiff, c.1908, is 71cm (28in) high, but all the years of being loved and played with have taken their toll. His stuffing has collapsed and he no longer stands to his full height. His fabric has holes in it and is now very fragile. This kind of bear will need a lot of very skilful restoration.

sometimes hidden away on the floor. Rummaging through these boxes is nearly always worthwhile and, armed with some knowledge, a bargain can often be spotted. These mixed boxes can be bought quite reasonably, and it is great fun when you arrive home and start cleaning the bears to discover if you have uncovered any treasures.

Remember when buying at auction that there is a commission to pay on top of the hammer price, and that can be a hefty 15 per cent plus VAT. Also, the descriptions in the catalogue are not always accurate, so it is best to acquire some knowledge of bears before you start. Auction rooms can be quite intimidating places, especially the large, general antiques sales, and for a beginner there are a few things to keep in mind: make sure that you have viewed properly; and decide on the top price you wish to pay to and stick to it, to avoid getting carried away during the bidding.

BUILDING A COLLECTION

An interesting aspect to collecting is the development of your interests over the years. You may start by collecting new bears only, but then find that you have a growing interest in old bears as well, or vice versa. Or you may focus on just one type of bear: many collectors develop a special liking for a certain make of vintage bear, while others collect particular bear artists or a range of bears from the same era, which makes for a very interesting collection. Vintage bears

MINIATURE BEARS
These miniature bears are from the 1930s; the bear on the right is by Steiff and the other is by an unknown maker. Forming a collection of miniature bears is fascinating. They can look great grouped together and displayed in a glass cabinet and they take up very little space.

sometimes come with their history, and if you are very lucky even a photograph of the original owner (see pp.82–5). These bears can form a fascinating collection, although they can be difficult to find, and they are always more valuable than a bear without its history. What is exciting about collecting bears is that there is so much to choose from, and you have the freedom to select the direction in which you want your collection to go.

MINIATURE BEARS

If you have limited space for a collection in your home, then you may want to consider miniature bears. Many bear artists make exquisite miniatures and they sell out very quickly. If you want a specific bear it is often advisable to place an order, but you may have to wait quite a long time for it. Miniatures are also available in vintage form: one of the most famous makers of old miniature bears is the German firm of Schuco, which made a wide range of miniature bears and novelties. Some collectors specialize in Schuco miniatures (see pp.52–3) but Steiff also made some delightful miniature bears. During World War I various companies produced soldier bears, made in patriotic colours, as little good luck mascots to be placed in soldiers' top pockets. There are many charming miniature old bears by unidentified makers that can be found too, so if you are short of space you can still create an exciting collection using these small, characterful bears.

BUYING AND SELLING BEARS

You will always come across bears that you would like to add to your own collection, but of course no one has infinite space or money to carry on buying whatever takes their fancy. There will be bears in your collection that you would never sell, but sometimes the lure of a new face will tempt you to part with a bear that you are less fond of. This can be a good way of keeping a check on the size of your collection and will save you money too. Remember that it is always best to have a smaller, better-quality collection than a huge one with no order to it. If you are buying from a dealer it is quite possible that you can part-exchange a bear, or they may take it on sale or return. The other option is to put a bear in an auction, although there is no guarantee it will sell and there are commission charges to pay if you do succeed in selling it. A reserve should be put on the bear, so it cannot sell for a lower price than you would want. Some people prefer to sell to someone they know and collectors often trade among themselves.

Keeping a record of your collection is very important and if it is valuable it may need separate insurance. It is amazing how the value of a collection mounts up over a period of time, and even if you don't need separate insurance, you should always keep your receipts and take a separate photo of each bear. It is a good idea to buy an album and put the photo and the receipt together – that way a complete record of your bears and their value is always to hand, and if the worst happens and you have a fire, burglary or flood there will be no dispute with the insurance company. Remember old bears can rise in value, and you will need to update your insurance valuation regularly.

With such a wide variety of bears to choose from, to learn all there is to know will take a long time. But if you can decide what type of bear appeals and what is within your budget, then using a book such as this and handling as many bears as possible will provide you with specialist knowledge to help in recognizing dates and makers, and assist in finding teddy bears that are rare and unusual. There is always a thrill when a special bear is found, but remember to buy only what you like – it does not matter whether it is worth a lot or a little if it is going to give you pleasure for many years to come. Teddy bear collecting is a world of endless pleasure and fascination and the following chapters will help you to discover more about it.

POPULAR VINTAGE MAKERS The well-known makers of old bears such as Chiltern, Chad Valley and Merrythought, which made both these desirable bears, are very collectable. Examples of a maker's work from each era will form a wonderful collection, giving great pleasure and providing a very good investment.

PRICING INFORMATION

The values in this book are a guideline only, and may alter depending on the condition of the bear, its geographical location and market trends. The sterling/dollar conversion has been made at a rate of £1=$1.50, which should be adjusted as necessary to accord with current exhange rates.

VINTAGE BEARS

JOPI RED MUSICAL BEAR
This red bear, c.1920, is made by the Jopi factory in Nuremberg and is rare because of his pristine condition. He has wonderfully thick, long, curly red mohair that has not faded over the years; he also has a musical movement in his tummy. **Ht 41cm (16in),** £2,000–2,500 ($3,000–3,750)

BING

HOW TO RECOGNIZE A BING BEAR

• Early bears, *c.* 1910, have small ears set wide apart, black button eyes, small facial features, jointed arms and legs, curved paws and a swivel head.

• Bing bears' plump bodies are stuffed with wood wool; they have a hump and a tilt growler. They also have flat feet with felt pads and silk claw stitching.

• The early Bing bears are made in mohair and have a silver metal G.B.N. tag under the arm. The final seam, as on Steiff bears, is sewn up the front of the body.

• Bing was famous for both dressed and undressed mechanical bears. There were many variations – walking bears, skating bears, acrobatic bears and many more.

• There was a distinctive design in use on some of Bing's non-mechanical bears from 1910. The "all-in-one" ears design meant that the head and ears were cut from one piece of fabric.

• Some bears, *c.* 1920, have long, shaved muzzles and foot pads coming to a point at the heel. They appear to stand on tiptoe and always have glass eyes.

In 1865 the brothers Ignaz and Adolf Bing founded the Nuremberg Spielwarenfabrik Gebrüder Bing in 1865 and produced kitchenware and toys. The company was extremely successful and within two years was employing over 100 workers. It even extended its range to include typewriters and carburettors for motorcycles and cars. In 1895 Adolf Bing left the company and Ignaz became chairman. Bing began producing mechanical tin toys such as clockwork cars, trains, boats, tinplate animals and dolls' kitchens. Then, around 1907, it started to produce its first plush toys. The teddy bear boom was at its height and the company at the forefront of the market, Steiff (*see* pp.54–9), could hardly cope with the orders. Bing was a large and powerful company by then, employing 3,000 workers, so Steiff could hardly have been pleased when the first Bing bear appeared, carrying a metal button in its right ear with the initials G.B.N. (Gebrüder Bing Nuremberg) impressed on it.

EARLY BING BEAR
This bear is *c.*1910 and still has the silver button under her arm that increases her overall value. She is in excellent condition and has thick gold mohair and wood wool stuffing. Her small ears are set on the side of her wide head, which is very characteristic of early Bing bears. She has black shoe-button eyes and vertical nose stitching and her arms are long and curved with felt paw pads. She also has a tilt growler and her oval feet are, typically, lined with cardboard. Ht 56cm (22in), £3,000–4,000 ($4,500–6,000)

LABELS AND DESIGNS

Bing was taken to court by Steiff's formidable team of lawyers in 1908, and was forced to remove the button from the ear and refrain from using the advertising slogan "button in the ear", as Steiff had the legal right to those words. Bing then tried using a metal tag shaped like a signal in black, cream and red, clipped in the ear, but Steiff also rejected this. Bing therefore placed the button under the bears' arms. Steiff also took legal steps to stop Bing from using the words "button under the arm" and so by 1908 Bing had to use the words "G.B.N. tag under the arm". It is very rare to find a Bing bear carrying a signal tag – the silver button is more often found.

Early Bing bears were made of high-quality mohair and stuffed with wood wool (exelsior). They were also very Steiff-like in appearance, having humps and black button eyes. They came in three colours of mohair: dark brown, gold and white. As Bing had expertise in mechanical toys, it was not long before they decided to "breathe life into their bears" by making them move. As early as 1908 a bear made in four sizes was available with a clockwork mechanism that made its head move from side to side. This time Bing made sure they protected themselves with patents and registered designs. Early mechanical bears from Bing can be found with a tin button on the body with "DRPDIVDRGM" written on a red background. These letters indicate that Bing had applied for a patent.

Bing made many wonderful and innovative walking and tumbling bears. One such early mechanical bear, advertised from 1910, was an upright bear holding a ball made from painted metal. It moved around in a circle pushing the ball. A rollerskating bear with a forward and backward movement was made too – a design that Schuco copied in the 1950s. These Bing bears, made of short bristle mohair in gold and brown and hard stuffed with wood wool, are extremely collectable today.

IDENTIFYING FEATURES

This large Bing paw has a felt pad and four claws sewn in black silk, which are not visible as they are hidden by the fur.

This silver button, with "G.B.N." set in a diamond design on it, was used from 1908 and was attached under each bear's left arm.

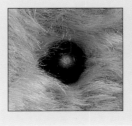

These black button eyes were used on early bears. Glass eyes with black pupils and orange painted backs replaced them.

The vertical stitching shown here was used only on the noses of bears that were 41cm (16in) or more.

BING

LATER RARE BEAR
Incredibly tall and extremely rare, this magnificent bear was made c.1916. He has long, thick golden mohair and brown glass eyes with black pupils. His shape is different to that of Bing's earlier bears, as he has a larger head and a longer shaved muzzle. His ears are set higher on his head but he still has the same stuffing, wood wool, as the earlier examples. However, his arms are shorter and not as curved.
Ht 81cm (32in), £8,000–10,000 ($12,000–15,000)

GOLDEN BROWN BING
This c.1928 bear has the blue B.W. tag under his arm that was used from 1927 until the factory closed in 1932. This particular bear is in excellent condition – even his tilt growler still works. His long, shaved muzzle has a wide smiling mouth running along the length of the snout, the large glass eyes have orange painted backs and the mohair is golden brown.
Ht 58cm (23in), £5,000–6,000 ($7,500–9,000)

CURLY MOHAIR

Dated c.1920, this white Bing has short curly mohair, a brown nose and the claw stitching typically used on white bears. All the larger bears, 41cm (16in) plus, have vertically stitched noses with a double border stitch, and long central stitches down to an inverted V-shaped mouth. The smaller bears have horizontal stitching with a single border stitch that is similar to that used by Steiff. **Ht 50cm (20in), £2,000–3,000 ($3,000–4,000)**

POST-WORLD WAR I

When Ignaz Bing died in 1918, his son Stephan took over the company. It had survived World War I intact, although production was reduced. The company name was changed to Bing Werke and from then on the G.B.N. buttons were discontinued. Instead, circular metal tags on the wrist and body were used. These had "B.W." written on them and the logo included the words Germany or Bavaria. The colours of the metal tags changed through the years – the rarest tag is the white one as it was used only for a short time in 1919.

The 1920s were very successful years for the company. During this time the design of the jointed bears developed and changed; the catalogue from this era offers fully jointed and soft-stuffed bears in yellow, brown and white mohair. They came in various sizes – the smaller with squeakers and the larger with tilt growlers. Pull-along bears-on-wheels, some large enough for a child to ride on, were also popular. The larger of these bears had a pull voice box on their back, which was similar to those made by Steiff, and during this period the wonderful range of mechanical bears continued to be made.

In 1927 Stephan Bing and all other family members resigned from the company because Jewish firms were being discriminated against under Hitler's Nazi regime. New management was bought in and for a few years the company struggled on, but in 1932 it went into receivership and all the machinery was put up for auction.

BEAR-ON-WHEELS

This realistic bear is on metal wheels and has the red B.W. tag on his front leg, which dates him from 1919. He has a hump back just like a real bear and a seam down the centre of his face. Bing bears-on-wheels are very hard to find so are quickly snapped up by collectors. **Ht 28cm (11in), £1,400–1,600 ($2,100–2,400)**

MINIATURE BING BEAR

This tiny bear, c.1920, is extremely rare. He has a metal frame covered in mohair and is pin jointed with no paw pads. Unusually, the red B.W. tag is in place under his arm, though on such a tiny bear it looks rather too big. It is interesting to note that this bear is similar to the Schuco Piccolo range (see p.52), and perhaps it is no coincidence that Heinrich Müller from Schuco worked for Bing between 1909 and 1912. **Ht 10cm (4in), £600–800 ($900–1,200)**

LONG-HAIRED BING

Made c.1920, this bear has the extra long mohair that was commonly used at the time. His eyes are glass with orange backs, he has a long shaved muzzle, his feet are long and slim with felt pads and his arms are straight. There is no tag in place but it is often possible to see a hole where the tag would have been. In this case it was positioned on the wrist. **Ht 46cm (18in), £2,000–3,000 ($3,000–4,500)**

IDENTIFYING FEATURES

Glass eyes were in general use after World War I but they were available earlier.

This red tag has B.W. written on it and was used from 1919 to 1927.

This metal tag was used from 1927 until 1932 on the wrist or under the arm.

CHAD VALLEY

HOW TO RECOGNIZE CHAD VALLEY BEARS

• Early bears are fully jointed and stuffed with kapok, and some very early ones have cork as a stuffing. They have a celluloid ID button used in the ear or upper torso.

• Early bears have eyes made of large amber and black glass, sewn through the head and finished with a knot. They have large flat ears set on the corners of the head and sewn over the facial seams.

• They have cardboard inserts in their large oval feet, which often have felt pads and a label stitched lengthways on them. They have four stitched claws on their paws and five on their feet. Some very early bears have cotton paw pads.

• All Chad Valley bears have prominent shaved muzzles, but the nose stitching varies: early bears have triangular-shaped noses with vertical stitching and a long horizontal stitch against the upper edge. In 1938 the triangular shape changed to a wide rectangular nose called a bound nose, with vertical stitches topped by one horizontal stitch.

There is little known about the origins of this company but in 1850 two brothers, Joseph and Alfred Johnson, started up their own business in George Street, Birmingham, and called it Johnson Brothers. Their speciality was stationery. In 1897 Joseph, who was by then running the company with the help of his son, moved to a new factory in the village of Harborne, near Birmingham. The company's name was changed at this time to Johnson Brothers Harborne and the factory was known as the Chad Valley works, after the Chad stream that runs nearby. The company adopted Chad Valley as their trademark in 1897 and extended the range to include cardboard games. They prospered and soon began producing soft toys. When Chad Valley took over Chiltern (*see* pp.24–7) in 1967 most of the production moved to Pontypool in Wales. However, during the recession in the 1970s the company was hit hard and in 1978 was taken over by Pallitoy. Woolworths bought the Chad Valley name in 1988 and soft toy production moved to the Far East.

TYPICAL CHAD BEAR
This bear from 1929 is in pristine condition. He has an appealing expression made by quite wide-set eyes, a triangular-shaped nose and a wide smiling mouth stretching across his shaved muzzle. His mohair is thick and curly and he is stuffed with kapok, which makes him soft and light, unlike some very early Chad Valley bears that were hard stuffed with cork. Hexagonal paper labels sewn to the body were used in the 1920s, with the words "Aerolite" and "I.S.A." placed just above the registered trademark. **Ht 50cm (20in), £800–1,000 ($1,200–1,500)**

BEAR WITH BUTTON & LABEL

This 1930 Chad Valley bear has a blue celluloid button in his left ear with the words "Chad Valley British Hygienic Toys" written on it. This bear has the typical Chad Valley shape, with large flat ears, a shaved muzzle and a slight hump. The paw pads are made of tan felt and the red and white embroidered label is placed on the right foot. **Ht 50cm (20in), £600–800 ($900–1,200)**

PRE-WORLD WAR II

The first teddy bear to be made by the company appeared in the 1914–15 catalogue. This bear was available in 13 sizes and five different fabrics. The beginning of World War I changed the toy business in Britain completely, as toys imported from German companies such as Steiff and Bing were banned. This meant that English manufacturers could step in to fill the gap, and Chad Valley did just that. It outgrew its factory in Harborne as a result and so, in 1919, acquired another property nearby in order to accommodate the printing for the boxes and the labels for the games. Another new site was then founded in Wellington, Shropshire, and in 1920 the Wrekin Toy Works were opened specifically for the production of their teddy bears. It was at this time that the name of the company was changed to the Chad Valley Co. Ltd.

Alfred Johnson became the managing director in 1904 and he worked until 1936. There was a big expansion of business in the years between the wars, with a wide range of games and toys made. Teddy bears and soft toys appeared in the catalogues during this period and many of the bears were stuffed with kapok and came in various fabrics with many new designs. But the classic Chad Valley teddy bear remained the same for many years through the 1920s and '30s. There were also novelty bears made, such as the Rainbow Tubby bear – an unusual standing clown bear (see p.79).

Fabric dolls were a large part of production. The Bambina line came out in 1927 and, in 1930, the first Royal doll of Princess Elizabeth appeared. On the bear front, the Magna series of bears were started around 1930. These were made in mohair and had horizontal nose stitching, which gave them a distinctive look. The company also produced coloured bears made in art silk and mohair. In 1931 the company bought Peacock and Co. Ltd. toy makers and brought out a bear with the Peacock label on it. At the height of its success, Chad Valley was granted the Royal Warrant of Appointment in 1938, as toy makers to Her Majesty the Queen.

EARLY BEAR

This early Chad Valley, c.1925, is hard stuffed with wood wool and has small cupped ears set on a triangular head. He has a prominent muzzle and, unusually, horizontal nose stitching. He is made with very short pile mohair, while his paw pads are made of cotton with no stitching. Similar bears have been found with the Chad Valley button on the upper torso, but this one has lost his. **Ht 41cm (16in), £300–500 ($450–750)**

PRISTINE BEAR

This bear made c.1935 is in mint condition – even his ribbon is original and his rich gold mohair is unfaded. This reveals that he has never been played with, which is rather sad. However, he would be prized by collectors because of his top condition. **Ht 50cm (20in), £1,000–1,500 ($1,500–2,250)**

IDENTIFYING FEATURES

This nose dates from the 1920s and has been found on bears that have the Aerolite button on them.

Yellow and black eyes are found on bears c.1925–29.

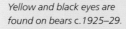

This white celluloid button, with "The Chad Valley British Toys" on it was used in the 1930s up until the start of World War II in 1939.

This wider, thicker stitched nose followed on from the earlier version.

CHAD VALLEY

MINT-CONDITION BEAR
It is usually very rare to find a bear that has never been played with, but this is another example of just that. This c.1955 bear even has his original paper label and ribbon and his golden shaggy mohair is as thick and glossy as the day he left the factory. His head is wide, his glass eyes are a reddish brown and he has the wide, bound stitched nose typical of Chad Valley bears. The label is stitched to his right paw pad, which is made of dark brown rexine.
Ht 51cm (20in), £1,000–1,200 ($1,500–1,800)

POST-1953 BEARS
Chad Valley bears are easier to date than other bears, because they usually have a label attached to one foot. After 1938, when the company was granted the royal warrant, all labels carried the royal coat of arms with the words "Toy Makers to Her Majesty the Queen" written on them. After the coronation of Elizabeth II in 1953, the words changed to "Queen Mother", as is written on the labels of these two c.1956 bears. **Left: ht 36cm (14in), £350–450 ($525–675). Right: ht 33cm (13in), £250–350 ($375–525)**

WORLD WAR II & BEYOND

The outbreak of World War II affected toy production dramatically and the factory's output was turned to supporting the war effort in a wide variety of ways. The Wrekin Works were easily transformed into a children's clothes manufacturers as their equipment was set up to take fabric. The woodworking machines that had made games became busy making instrument cases and wood containers for gun barrels. The company carried on making toys and games, which were sent to the forces and used in military hospitals.

At the end of the war Chad Valley recovered rapidly and the post-war period was a time of expansion. It also resulted in changes in the materials used for making teddy bears. During the 1950s plastic eyes and moulded noses were used on some bears. Safety eyes that were locked in with washers also appeared, as did synthetic fabrics.

The company began producing character bears from TV and radio. A replica of Harry Corbett's popular TV character Sooty (*see* p.130) came out in 1954, together with his friend Sweep. Another favourite was Toffee, a character from the BBC radio programme "Listen with Mother". Washable bears, made from synthetic fabrics and filled with plastic foam, became more popular during the 1960s and 1970s.

CUBBY BEAR
This unusual little bear, c.1955, is made of wool plush in two colours – caramel and cream. He has glass eyes and ears that are lined with cream plush, set wide apart. He is fully jointed and has short straight arms with downward-facing rexine paw pads that have three black stitched claws. His legs are chubby and his feet large and oblong with five stitched claws. **Ht 36cm (14in), £250–350 ($375–525)**

BLENDED MOHAIR BEAR
This bear, made in the 1960s, is a blend of mohair and nylon. This gives him a different texture to those of pure mohair – he is more bobbly than silky to the touch. Chad Valley also made a fully jointed nylon version of this bear in white and lemon. During this period washable bears in nylon plush were very popular. This bear is made in a classic Chad Valley design, having wide-apart ears and a black bound nose. **Ht 36cm (14in), £100–200 ($150–300)**

TOFFEE BEAR
Toffee was based on a character from a series of children's stories that were broadcast on a BBC radio programme called "Listen with Mother". The knitted red hat and scarf are original features of the Toffee bear. His large flat ears are set on the side of his head, which has a high domed forehead and a flat muzzle. He is made in mohair and has short arms with rexine pads. Made c.1954 the Toffee bear is very collectable and usually hard to find. **Ht 25cm (10in), £400–500 ($600–750)**

IDENTIFYING FEATURES

This label dates from after 1953 as it has the words "Queen Mother" on it.

This "Hygienic Toys" paper label was tied around the neck of late 1950s bears.

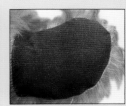
Rexine paw pads, used in the 1950s, have a distinctive suede-like appearance.

CHILTERN

- Chiltern bears usually have large brown glass eyes, although in early bears clear glass with black pupils was used. The head is normally stuffed with wood wool and the body with kapok, while the ears are cupped and set at a slight angle.

- The body of a Chiltern bear is fully jointed and has long arms. The paws are spoon shaped and incorporate cotton pads (velvet pads on early bears). The claw stitching on the paws is usually of black silk. Later bears are often unjointed and made of synthetic fabrics.

- Bears are made of short, clipped or long mohair. Shaggy, coloured mohair was popular during the 1920s and '30s.

- Bears made after World War II have much flatter faces and their arms and legs are also shorter. Plastic noses were introduced in the 1960s.

In 1881 two brothers named Josef and Gabriel Eisenmann founded Eisenmann and Co. in Bavaria. It began as an export agency dealing in fancy goods and a small amount of toys, but when the company opened offices in London the business grew. Just prior to World War I they became one of the biggest importers of toys from Germany. They were one of the founders of the British toy industry and were the first company to introduce the teddy bear to Britain. Leon Rees had been born in Germany but moved to London in 1900 to be a partner in Eisenmann and Co. He married Josef's daughter Maude in 1908 and in the same year established the Chiltern Toy Works in Chesham, Buckinghamshire. Rees was very impressed by the teddy bears he had seen in Germany and it is thought that as early as 1908 he suggested to the manufacturer J.K. Farnell (presumably because Chiltern were not interested in making bears at this time) that it should begin making its own teddy bears, as it was much cheaper than importing them from Germany.

TWO MASTER TEDDIES
Master Teddy was the first ever Chiltern bear, made c.1915. As a result he is very rare and highly collectable. He has a large round head with small ears and big glass "googly" eyes, his nose has vertical stitching and he has a smiling embroidered mouth with long end stitches and a small pink felt tongue. All of these distinct features combine to give him a most unique appearance. He has a linen body with mohair feet and hands, and is charmingly dressed in felt trousers and a cotton shirt. Left: ht 25cm (10in), £1,500–1,800 ($2,250–2,700). Right: 20cm (8in), £800–1,200 ($1,200–1,800)

EARLY HUGMEE BEAR

Hugmee bears were the most popular of all the Chiltern bears; they first appeared in 1923 and were produced for many years. This bear has all the characteristics of the early Hugmee – a large head stuffed with wood wool, glass eyes and body of short pile mohair. His arms are plump but taper down to the paws, which have cotton pads. The legs are quite thick at the top, but he has narrow ankles.
Ht 64cm (25in),
£400–600 ($600–900)

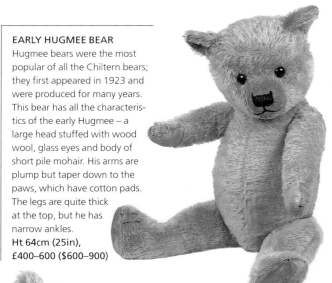

LUXURIOUS MOHAIR

This Hugmee bear is made of luxurious shaggy mohair, which was typical of those produced in the late 1930s. The heavy triangular-shaped head on the soft kapok body causes the head of such bears to droop onto their chest. Many of these early bears have clear glass eyes, which are sewn in and tied with a final stitch at the back of the head, although brown glass eyes were also used at this time. Ht 71cm (28in), £700–900 ($1,050–1,350)

PRE-WORLD WAR II

In 1912 Chiltern was mainly producing wooden toys and fabric dolls with china heads, but in 1915 their first teddy bear, Master Teddy, appeared. Master Teddy had glass googly eyes and was dressed in trousers and a jacket; his head and limbs were made of mohair and he had a fabric body.

Then, in 1919, Josef Eisenmann died, leaving complete control of the business to Leon Rees. In 1920 Rees formed a partnership with his friend Harry Stone and together they formed H.G. Stone Ltd., making soft toys at the Chiltern Toy Works in Chesham. By then the factory had already moved from its old site to a larger building. Harry Stone was a respected figure in the toy trade and he had very broad experience, as he had been a former director of J.K. Farnell.

In 1921 the company opened a second factory in Grove Road, Tottenham, north London. The production from this factory was done under the name of Leon Rees and Co., as the famous Chiltern Toys trademark was not officially registered until 1924, when the Hugmee teddy bears were first introduced. That particular range was very successful and continued to be made right up until 1967.

In 1929 a new factory was built at Bernhard Road in Tottenham, and this was also named the Chiltern Toy Works. All production was moved over there from the old Tottenham factory. During the 1930s there were many new innovations, such as the Bellows Musical bear that played a number of different tunes, Silky Teddy, a skater bear and bears of various unusual colours. Chiltern's Cubby bear was also introduced at this time.

In 1934 Harry Stone died. The company continued to produce bears, but when World War II began in 1939, production ceased at Chesham. Some staff continued to commute to the London factory, where a few toys were still made during the war using whatever materials were available.

EARLY FACTORY PHOTOGRAPH

This unique photograph, taken in 1925, shows the assembly line at the Chiltern factory in Waterside, Chesham. Production had moved to this site from Bellingham Road in 1920 and the factory remained at its new location until 1940, when toy making ceased and the building was turned over to be used for the war effort.

IDENTIFYING FEATURES

This is a typical shaved muzzle found on Chiltern bears – the nose stitching incorporates long, upward end stitches.

Larger Chiltern bears have big oval feet that are lined with cardboard inserts to help keep their shape.

This cupped ear has been sewn to the facial seam and is set at an angle on the corner of the bear's head.

The velvet pads that taper toward the tip have four claws (not visible here).

CHILTERN

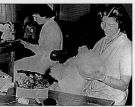
TWO CHILTERN HUGMEES

These late 1940s bears demonstrate the change in design that occurred during and after World War II, as materials became difficult to obtain. The face became much flatter and the nose stitching was changed to a shield shape without the long end stitches. The bears are made of gold mohair and their arms and legs are shorter and thinner than before. The feet are also smaller and the pads are covered in rexine, which was often used on British bears of this period. **Left:** ht 28cm (11in), £150–200 ($225–300). **Right:** ht 36cm (14in), £200–300 ($300–450)

GOLDEN HUGMEE

This Hugmee bear, c.1955, has an unshaved muzzle, which is characteristic of the period. His round ears are sewn into the facial seam and the brown and black glass eyes are set on the bridge of his nose. His long arms are thick and taper down to the pads, which are made of velvet and have four claws stitched over them. His chubby legs end in pointed feet, with thin cardboard inserts and black stitched claws. **Ht 71cm (28in), £300–400 ($450–600)**

POST-WORLD WAR II

After World War II a new factory was opened, in 1947, on a large site near Pontypool in Wales. The chief designer here was Madeleine Biggs. In 1957 Madeleine left the firm to go to South Africa and Pamela Williams (who became Pamela Howells) joined as an assistant designer, aged 17 years. Pamela eventually took over as chief designer and one of her first designs in that capacity was Chiltern's famous Teddy on a Bike. This was a great success and was made right up to the 1960s. The company's most famous bear, the Hugmee, continued to be made throughout the war and beyond. Gold mohair was the most popular colour after World War II, but coloured mohair, such as bright pink, was also used, and in the 1950s bears were made in white, blue and pink nylon fur.

There were many different designs made during the 1950s and '60s: bears with musical boxes inside them; the Ting-a-ling Bruin that had a mechanism inside that made a jingling sound; the Cubby bear; a standing bear with a musical movement inside and also a large range of animals and dolls. Unjointed bears were introduced, some of which were made of mohair but increasingly synthetic fabrics were replacing mohair. In 1960 Chiltern made the washable Chiltern toy series, which included unjointed bears made entirely of nylon plush and bears stuffed with the one-piece fairy foam filling.

The Chesham factory remained the centre of production for Chiltern's teddy bears until 1960, when the factory closed and all production moved to Pontypool in Wales. Chiltern bears were always wonderfully made, using high-quality materials. Of the 350 dedicated and talented employees who worked at the Pontypool factory, many of them started directly from school and stayed with the company for many years.

Leon Rees died in 1963 and in 1964 the Chiltern and Rees companies were taken over by the Dunbee Combex group. Eventually, in 1967, it became a subsidiary of Chad Valley (see p.20) and for a while the bears bore a label saying "Chad Valley Chiltern".

WASHABLE BEARS

The Musical Bruin, with his white muzzle and chest and black plastic nose, was originally made in the 1950s in mohair. This 1960s version is made in nylon plush and has plastic safety eyes. His body is unjointed except for the head and he stands on large oval feet that have cardboard inserts. The smaller Chiltern bear in front of him is also made in nylon plush and is foam filled. These safe, washable bears were popular in the 1960s. **Back: ht 36cm (14in), £60–80 ($90–120). Front: ht 25.5cm (10in), £40–50 ($60–75)**

CHAD VALLEY CHILTERN BEAR

This is an example of a very late Chad Valley Chiltern bear, made in 1968 just before the Chiltern name vanished for ever. This bear has nylon fur and is unjointed. He incorporates a one-piece filling known as "fairy foam", which made him fully washable. Fairy foam was used from the 1950s in many soft toys and was either moulded or chopped into shape. He has a moulded plastic nose and amber and black plastic locked-in safety eyes, which have an integral shank forming a screw, locked in place by a washer. **Ht 30cm (12in), £75–150 ($125–225)**

IDENTIFYING FEATURES

Chad Valley Chiltern labels were used by the company after 1967, which is when Chiltern was taken over by Chad Valley. However, this particular label was only in use for a short time.

This blue and white Chiltern label was used in the 1950s. If a label is missing, there is often a mark to indicate where it once was.

Chiltern originally used this moulded plastic nose, dating from 1960, on a toy dog with wheels, before using it on its bears.

DEAN'S RAG BOOK CO.

HOW TO RECOGNIZE A DEAN'S BEAR

• Early bears from the 1920s were fully jointed, made with mohair and stuffed with wood wool. From the early 1930s bears were also made in artificial silk and stuffed with kapok and wood wool.

• Many bears from the 1920s and '30s had shaved muzzles with embroidered black noses incorporating long downward end stitches. Some also had a silver ID button in their ear.

• The Tru-to-Life bear (*see* p.31) was made in three colours – white, black and honey. It also has distinctive moulded rubber paws and feet.

In 1953 this catalogue was published in order to celebrate 50 years of the company.

The Dean's Rag Book Co. Ltd. was founded in 1903 and based in Fleet Street, London. It is the oldest surviving British toy manufacturer. The company first produced a "rag" children's book that was printed on calico. It was washable and virtually indestructible and proved to be a huge success. In fact their trademark, designed by artist Stanley Berkley, shows a bulldog and a terrier tearing at a rag book. In 1905 the company introduced their Knockabout toy sheets, which were printed on cotton with the pieces ready to cut out and sew together. In 1908 the Knockabout teddy bear was added to the range. By 1911 bears were made in printed cotton but very few of these have survived to today. The company prospered at this time, mainly due to the demand for the Knockabout toys, rag books and printed teddy bears. This resulted in them moving to larger premises at the Elephant and Castle in south-east London in 1912. By the late 1930s they had outgrown these premises too. A new factory was planned at Merton, south-west London, on land that had once belonged to Lord Nelson.

ART SILK BEAR
This gold bear is made in artificial silk. He is in excellent original condition and has even retained his ribbon and bell. He is stamped on the foot with the Dean's logo that incorporates fighting dogs, and would originally have had the triangular A1 paper label tied around his neck. This bear, c.1930, is an example of one of the A1 first-grade bears made; he came in eight sizes.
Ht 56cm (22in),
£1,500–1,800
($2,250–2,700)

BLUE ART SILK BEAR

Made c.1930, this bear is also an A1 first-grade bear. He is made out of artificial silk, which was first used for making soft toys in 1929. This material was offered in three colours – gold, rose pink and saxe blue. This bear's body and head is stuffed with wood wool and his limbs with kapok. His head is round and he has cupped ears sewn across the facial seam. **Ht 48cm (19in), £800–1,000 ($1,200–1,500)**

DISMAL DESMOND

Dismal Desmond was a comic strip character in the 1920s and was made as a soft toy by Dean's. This example is c.1925. He is made in velvet and has the Dean's logo printed on his neck. Dismal Desmonds were also made in brushed cotton and came in a sitting position. His counterpart, Cheerful Desmond, was not successful so few were made and these are very rare today. **Ht 15cm (6in), £150–250 ($225–375)**

PINK MOHAIR BEAR

This pink bear, c.1930, is faded at the front, but from the back he still shows the original bright pink colour. He is hard stuffed with wood wool and has a silver button in his left ear with the Dean's trademark on it. His black embroidered nose is horizontally stitched and he has glass eyes. His paw pads are made of cotton fabric and they do not have any claw stitching. **Ht 30cm (12in), £500–700 ($750–1,050)**

WORLD WAR I & BEYOND

During World War I, when German imports were banned, Dean's brought out their first plush teddy, which appeared in a catalogue in 1915 under the "Kuddlemee" brand name. These included Master and Miss Bruno – dressed bears offered in either gold or white plush and available in three sizes – and an undressed bear with a ribbon and bell that was called the British Bear. The Kuddlemee range also included other soft toys such as ducks, cats, an elephant and a rabbit. Dean's were also famous for their dolls with moulded faces, and these first appeared during World War I.

In 1922 the first plush teddy bear appeared with a Dean's logo. From then on new designs appeared throughout the 1920s, and large-scale production really began. In 1922 the A1 label first appeared. This was a triangular paper label that was used on dolls and bears together with the Dean's logo. The "Evripoze" joints were patented by Dean's and used in its A1 Bendy Bear. This bear was filled with kapok and fitted with the joints, which allowed for greater flexibility of movement. In 1925 there were two grades of A1 bear, which were both filled with wood wool, were fully jointed and came in 14 sizes. However, by 1926 the A1 first-grade bears were stuffed with kapok and the cheaper second-grade examples were stuffed with wood wool. By the late 1920s most A1 bears were offered in various colours, such as pink and blue, but the second-grade ones were only available in gold. During this period Dean's used the synthetic fabric art silk, which allowed them to extend the range of colours they could offer.

Bears have always played an important part of Dean's production, but in the years leading up to World War II other characters and novelties began to appear, such as Pluto, Popeye, and Mickey and Minnie Mouse, which overtook the teddy bear in popularity.

IDENTIFYING FEATURES

This vertically stitched, silk-embroidered nose has long downward end stitches. Such noses were used on the A1 bears.

This glass eye, c.1930, has a black pupil and painted back. The eye is sewn through to the back of the head and finished with a knot.

Velvet paw pads are often worn away, revealing the cotton backing. Some Dean's paws also have four black stitched claws.

This c.1930 silver button was placed in bears' left ears. It is impressed with "Dean's Rag Book Co. Ltd".

DEAN'S RAG BOOK CO.

This printed Dean's fabric label was in use between the 1920s and 1955. It was usually sewn onto the bears' right foot pad. Each bear would also have had a paper label around its neck that incorporated the famous Dean's logo of the two dogs tearing at a rag book.

MOUSE-EARED BEARS
These are so-called because they have round heads and their ears are set on the sides. The larger bear has plastic eyes, which dates him after 1947. The bear on the right has glass eyes and is c. 1938. These bears are both fully jointed and made in mohair. The mouse-eared design was produced from the 1930s until the 1950s.
Left: ht 53cm (21in), £400–500 ($600–750). **Right:** ht 41cm (16in), £500–600 ($750–900)

LARGE DEAN'S BEAR
Dating from 1938, this bear has a very distinctive design. He has a large triangular head with cupped ears set on the corners. His brown and black glass eyes have wire shanks and are sewn in, and his nose is large and oblong with vertical stitching. His hump is quite small and his arms are thick and rather short, while his legs are chubby and end in felt paw pads. **Ht 68cm (27in), £600–800 ($900–1,200)**

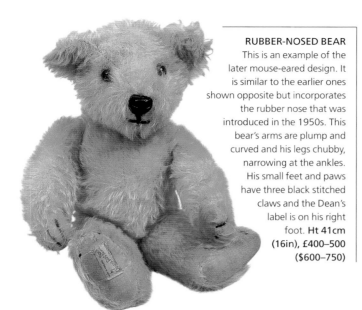

RUBBER-NOSED BEAR
This is an example of the later mouse-eared design. It is similar to the earlier ones shown opposite but incorporates the rubber nose that was introduced in the 1950s. This bear's arms are plump and curved and his legs chubby, narrowing at the ankles. His small feet and paws have three black stitched claws and the Dean's label is on his right foot. **Ht 41cm (16in), £400–500 ($600–750)**

TRU-TO-LIFE BEAR
The Tru-to-Life bear was designed by Sylvia Wilgos. This example is c.1955 and is unjointed. The bear's legs are attached to the front of the body and are stuffed with wood wool and kapok. The arms and legs are very floppy and the paws and claws are made of moulded rubber. The face is also made of rubber, with acrylic mohair stretched over it. **Ht 56cm (22in), £1,800–2,000 ($2,700–3,000)**

CHILDSPLAY TOY BEAR
This bear, c.1965, has locked-in plastic safety eyes and the heart-shaped Dean's Childsplay Toy Ltd swing label actually has a spare eye attached to it. This label dates him to the period when the factory was at Rye. He is made in mohair and stuffed with chipped foam. His paw pads are of a synthetic fabric and they do not have claw stitching. **Ht 41cm (16in), £200–300 ($300–450)**

WORLD WAR II & BEYOND

The Merton factory in south-west London was opened in 1936 but production never really got into full swing because of the outbreak of World War II. Instead the factory was turned over to manufacturing Bren gun covers, Mae Wests and other items to help the war effort.

After the war, recovery was slow due to staff shortages and lack of materials. It was not until 1948 that the first post-war catalogue came out. This included two ranges of bears called Golden Teddies; one range came in short pile mohair in three colours and the second in curly mohair. In 1949 a polar bear at London Zoo gave birth to a cub, which aroused great public interest and led Dean's to make a soft toy version of Ivy, the mother, in white mohair holding Brumas the cub (made in white wool).

By the 1950s teddy bears had once again become an important part of the Dean's range and in 1952 Sylvia Wilgos joined the firm as a designer. She is famous for her Tru-to-Life bears, which were introduced in the mid-1950s. She had been inspired by the bears she had spent time sketching at London Zoo. The resulting realistic bear had unique paw pads moulded in rubber, and came in three colours.

In 1956 the company needed to reduce overheads and so they moved from the Merton factory to a new location in Rye, East Sussex. A subsidiary company called Childsplay was also formed and from 1956 all bears had the printed "Childsplay Toys" label sewn inside their right arm joint. This label was used until 1965 when it was changed to "Dean's Childsplay Toys Ltd.". During the 1960s unjointed bears were made from synthetic fabrics and Dean's were the first British company to make bears from a nylon material called Brinylon.

Meanwhile, three former directors of Chiltern established a soft toy company in Wales in 1965 called Gwentoys. In 1967 they formed an association with Dean's and started to make some of Dean's bears. In 1972 the two companies merged and in 1980 the Dean's factory in Rye closed and all production was transferred to Wales, where bears continued to be successfully produced. Dean's was finally taken over in 1987 by Neil and Barbara Miller and in 1991 they brought out their first limited edition collectors' bear. Dean's is still flourishing today (*see* p.95).

IDENTIFYING FEATURES

This vertical black nose stitching, which comes down to a black, stitched, curved mouth on a shaved muzzle, was used on the mouse-eared bear from the 1930s.

The black moulded rubber nose was first used in the 1950s. Along with an embroidered inverted T-shaped mouth, it continued to be used on later bears.

J.K. FARNELL

HOW TO RECOGNIZE AN EARLY FARNELL BEAR

• Large bears have clear glass eyes but smaller ones usually have black button eyes. Most bears have quite large cupped ears set on the corner of their head but they can also sometimes have larger, flatter ears set on the side.

• The prominent muzzle of early bears is shaved and the nose vertically stitched in silk floss with long upward end stitches. Most of the mohair used is long and silky and is of very high quality.

• The paw pads can be made of felt but sometimes cotton twill is used. Some bears have distinctive webbed paw stitching with five long stitches radiating out from the centre. This design is very different to that used by other makers.

• The size of hump can vary but it is usually rounder than in Steiff bears. The long, curved arms taper towards the wrist and the legs are thick and chubby with narrow ankles and big feet.

J.K. Farnell was a family concern that was founded by John Kirby Farnell in the Notting Hill area of London in about 1840. The company specialized in making small household items such as pin cushions, decorative felt pen wipers and tea cosies. When John Kirby Farnell died his son and daughter, Henry and Agnes, moved the business to Elm House – a large 18th-century building situated on Acton Hill, west London, which had a small factory building in its garden where they established a soft toy company. As the demand for Farnell toys grew, the company became too large for this building and an extension was built in 1921. This was known as the Alpha works and Alpha became Farnell's trademark from that moment on. In 1925 Farnell introduced their range of Anima wheeled toys. Agnes Farnell died in 1928 and production moved to a new east London showroom.

TYPICAL EARLY BEAR
This Farnell bear, c.1912, has cupped ears set on the corners of his triangular head. He also has a long muzzle with a black stitched nose. Many of the early small Farnell bears show similarities to Steiff and this bear is no exception. He has plump, long, curved arms that reach down past his feet and his paw pads lack the distinctive Farnell webbed stitching (this is true of other small-sized Farnells). He has a chubby rounded body and is stuffed with wood wool. Early bears may also have horsehair stuffing, mainly around the growler.
Ht 43cm (17in),
£1,000–1,500
($1,500–2,250)

TWO SMALL FARNELLS

These two early bears are unusual because of their small size. The one on the left is c.1910, the other is c.1915. The left bear has the blond mohair typical of Farnell. His nose stitching has two long upward end stitches, his ears are large and he has flat black button eyes, unique to early Farnells. The bear on the right has a shaved muzzle and round button eyes. **Both bears: ht 23cm (9in), £500–700 ($750–1,050) each**

TWO WORLD WAR I BEARS

These two Farnells are from the World War I period. Growlers have been found in them with the words "Made in Britain by British labour". The curly blonde mohair on both is typical of Farnell bears. The ears are set on the corners of the rounded heads, the eyes are clear glass with black pupils and the bodies have distinctive humped backs. **Left: ht 48cm (19in), £1,500–2,000 ($2,250–3,000). Right: ht 43cm (17in), £1,400–1,800 ($2,100–2,700)**

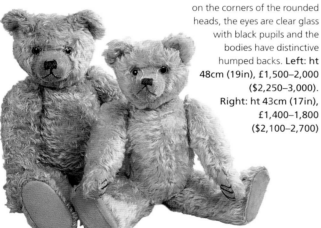

BEAR WITH SHORT MOHAIR

This bear, which is c.1918, has amber and black glass eyes. His large ears are set at a distinct angle on the side of his head, which is a characteristic of some Farnell bears but not all. His long arms reach down past his feet and his paw pads are made of felt. His golden mohair is slightly shorter than that found on some of the earlier bears. **Ht 64cm (25in), £1,800–2,000 ($2,700–3,000)**

EARLY DESIGNS

Early toys were made using rabbit skins as well as the more usual fabrics. J.K. Farnell is said to have made the first British teddy bear around 1908, but it is possible that bears actually appeared two years before. Early Farnell bears, with their black button eyes, large feet and long arms, are similar to Steiff bears and can be easily confused.

With the outbreak of World War I there was an increased demand for British toys and Farnell really took off. One of the directors during the pre-World War I years was Harry Stone who, in later years, went on to manufacture Chiltern toys (see p.25). The early Farnell bears were very distinctive, having webbed paw stitching, shaved muzzles, glass or button eyes, big feet with cardboard inserts and high-quality mohair. However, bears were only a part of Farnell's range as other animals and dolls were made as well.

Farnell was considered to be very innovative and its designs novel and imaginative. Sybil Kemp and Agnes Farnell were two of the early designers to work for the company. Popular designs included the wonderful Alpha bear (see pp.34–5), introduced in 1908, and Pip, Squeak and Wilfred – cartoon characters whose sales rivalled those of the teddy bears. During the 1920s soft toys became fashion accessories and were taken along to many of the social events of the period. The demand for these adult toys was enormous and by 1926 Farnell was manufacturing large quantities of miniature toys.

In the early years Farnell bears were unmarked, but the paper label was introduced in 1925. This was a round card disc that had a metal rim with the words "Alpha Make" on it, and was attached to a bear's chest. In 1926 an embroidered label appeared with the words "Alpha Toy" in blue and white, which was attached to the bears' foot.

The Alpha bear changed design in the late 1920s. The muzzle was left unshaven and the webbed paw stitching discontinued. These later bears had large glass eyes and square stitched noses. A coloured Silkalite teddy bear, made in artificial silk in a wide variety of colours, was also introduced in 1929.

IDENTIFYING FEATURES

The large oval felt foot pads have cardboard inserts as well as four claws. Cotton pads were also used.

Round shiny button eyes are a distinctive feature used on smaller-sized early bears.

This is a paw pad from a smaller Farnell. These pads can cause confusion as they do not have Farnell's webbed paw stitching.

This paw pad has the five distinctive long stitches of Farnell bears.

J.K. FARNELL

ALPHA BEAR
This 1930 Alpha bear is made in luxurious white mohair. He has large round ears set on the corners of his head and dark glass eyes. His rectangular, bulbous, vertically stitched nose is made in a light-coloured silk that was often used on white bears. His paw pads are made in tan-coloured rexine and have silk claw stitching. White bears like this are hard to find in good condition as the mohair has often discoloured. Ht 71cm (28in), £2,000–3,000 ($3,000–4,500)

RARE-COLOURED BEARS
These two bears are examples of the rare-coloured Farnells that were popular during the 1920s. The bear on the right has thick lilac mohair, still unfaded, and his ears are set at an angle on his head. The bear on the left is made in pale pink mohair, which has faded slightly, and he has large glass eyes, small ears and light-coloured nose stitching. Left: ht 25cm (10in), £1,200–1,500 ($1,800–2,250). Right: ht 30cm (12in), £2,000–2,500 ($3,000–3,750)

LATER ALPHA BEAR

This gold mohair bear of 1938 still has the blue and white Alpha Farnell label on his foot. His paw pads are covered in rexine, which has worn revealing the cotton lining underneath. He has quite a prominent snout, with a square, vertically stitched nose, and large cupped ears. His arms are short and plump at the top, tapering down to the paws.
Ht 33cm (13in),
£200–300 ($300–450)

MOHAIR AND SYNTHETIC FABRIC

The c.1938 bear on the left is made in high-quality white mohair, which was used before World War II, and he also has a press squeaker in his tummy. The other bear is from 1950 and is an example of bears with synthetic fabric made to resemble golden mohair. He has oval feet with rexine pads, set on chubby little legs.

Left: ht 28cm (11in), £250–350 ($375–525). Right: ht 38cm (15in), £150–250 ($225–375)

1950 ALPHA BEAR

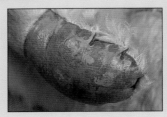

This wool plush bear has amber and black glass eyes and his head is quite large in comparison to his body, which is typical of post-World War II Farnell bears. His mouth stitching points downward, which gives him a rather serious expression. His body is quite straight, not plump like earlier bears. He is fully jointed with short stubby limbs and fairly small round feet with rexine pads.
Ht 36cm (14in),
£150–200 ($225–300)

DIFFICULT TIMES

The company grew through the 1920s and '30s but its toys were expensive because only high-quality materials were used. Also, due to over production, the company needed to expand its markets, so it opened showrooms in Paris and New York. This was how its export drive started. Farnell introduced a cheaper line, the Unicorn range, in 1931 and sold half a million of these toys in the first year.

In July 1934 a terrible fire destroyed the factory and all production was wiped out. A year later it reopened and continued to make Alpha toys under the relaunched Alpha label. The Unicorn range of toys had disappeared but instead a cheaper Alpha and Teddy series of bears was reintroduced. Cloth dolls were also made with the new machinery that had been installed and by 1939 there were 250 different doll designs.

New teddies appeared occasionally, such as the Chubby bear that came complete with cup and spoon, but in 1940 the factory was destroyed again, this time by the bombing that occurred during World War II. The company rebuilt the factory once more, but this time recovery was much more difficult because there was a general lack of materials during the post-war period, and the economic climate was poor. Cheaper foreign imports from the Far East also began to flood the market.

In the hopes of seeing an upturn in their fortunes, in 1959 Farnell built a second, smaller factory in Hastings to make toys for export, but within a few years the company was forced to downsize, and all business was transferred to Hastings from the larger London site. Alpha bears were still made in mohair and were still fully jointed but the design had become more economical. The arms and legs were shorter and the label had changed to a red, white and blue design. This label had the words "This is a quality soft toy made in Hastings, England" written on it. Farnell also made cheaper, unjointed toys in synthetic fabrics but these were poorly designed and badly made. In 1968 the company was bought out by a finance company and production ceased. The name was bought by Merrythought in 1996, which now produces high-quality replicas of the original Farnell bears (*see* p.97).

IDENTIFYING FEATURES

This blue and white embroidered label was used by the company from 1925 to 1945. The label was often sewn lengthways onto a bear's foot.

This rexine paw pad from the 1930s shows the four claws stitched across the edges of the pad. This replaced webbed stitching.

This label was used by Farnell between 1959, when the factory moved to Hastings, and 1968, when the factory closed.

INVICTA

• During the lifetime of the company the design of Invicta bears did not vary much. They are fully jointed and have a tilt growler or squeaker. Many of the bears also have large, clear glass eyes and the head is usually wide and rather flat.

• The bulbous, oblong nose has vertical stitching – it is created by pinching the plush together and overstitching it tightly. This is often done in light-coloured silk.

• Early bears have long arms and very large oval feet. The mohair used on some of them is long and bright gold, while the stuffing is wood wool and kapok.

• Bears were made in mohair and wool plush but after World War II synthetic fabrics were also popular.

• Paw pads are often made of rexine but can be velvet too. The larger bears often have stitched claws, but not always.

Two former employees of J.K. Farnell, G.E. Beer and T.B. Wright, established Invicta Toys on 1 January 1935. Wright had been a sales representative and Beer a director and designer at Farnell. Their own company was based at Sunbeam Road, Park Royal in north-west London. They decided to name it Invicta after the Latin word "Invicti", which means unconquerable and unbeaten. They employed about 300 staff and made a wide range of soft toys including, as well as bears, cats, dogs, rabbits, monkeys and many animals on wheels. In 1936 Beer bought out Wright and in the run-up to World War II he was very successful in making fully jointed bears that had glass eyes, were stuffed with wood wool and kapok and had extremely distinctive bulbous, stitched noses. However, production was reasonably short-lived and Invicta closed after just 20 years of business.

ALPACA PLUSH BEAR
This small Invicta bear, c.1936, is made of alpaca plush. He has a squeaker in his tummy but it no longer works, which often happens with older squeakers. The bear has rather large ears that are set on the side of his head and also has brown and black glass eyes. His fairly prominent muzzle has a turned-up nose with light brown stitching, his arms are long and his feet narrow. **Ht 20cm (8in), £300–400 ($450–600)**

PAIR OF INVICTA BEARS

These two bears dated c.1950 have big ears sewn into the facial seam. This design is actually very similar to that of J.K. Farnell and, with very little being known until recently about Invicta bears, many were wrongly identified as being Alpha Farnell bears. As Beer had worked as a designer for Farnell it is not surprising that such similarities do exist. **Left: ht 38cm (15in), £200–300 ($300–450). Right: ht 61cm (24in), £400–500 ($600–750)**

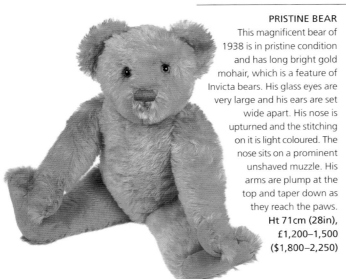

PRISTINE BEAR

This magnificent bear of 1938 is in pristine condition and has long bright gold mohair, which is a feature of Invicta bears. His glass eyes are very large and his ears are set wide apart. His nose is upturned and the stitching on it is light coloured. The nose sits on a prominent unshaved muzzle. His arms are plump at the top and taper down as they reach the paws. Ht 71cm (28in), £1,200–1,500 ($1,800–2,250)

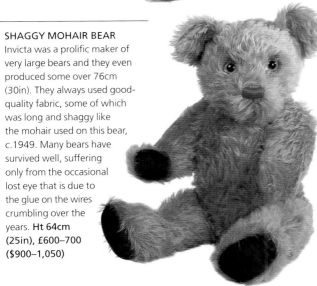

SHAGGY MOHAIR BEAR

Invicta was a prolific maker of very large bears and they even produced some over 76cm (30in). They always used good-quality fabric, some of which was long and shaggy like the mohair used on this bear, c.1949. Many bears have survived well, suffering only from the occasional lost eye that is due to the glue on the wires crumbling over the years. Ht 64cm (25in), £600–700 ($900–1,050)

WORLD WAR II & BEYOND

During World War II the factory's production was turned over to war work, making armaments, like so many other toy factories. At this time the majority of the workers left. However, the firm moved to a disused laundry in south Acton, London, taking a couple of employees with them, and carried on manufacturing toys, albeit a reduced amount. They were able to mark and cut out fabric and send it away to outworkers to be sewn up. This was returned and then stuffed and finished off and, in this way, a small selection of toys continued to be made during the war.

When the war was finally over Invicta moved back to a section of the old factory and by 1948 was employing a new workforce. Its export books were soon full with orders from department stores in the USA, Canada, Switzerland and Australia – Invicta bears are often found in these countries today. The bears were always of good quality and have been mistaken for Farnell bears (see pp.32–5) because the designs have similarities to Farnell's, as does the mohair that was used. Invicta's range included Teddy, Grizzle and Sammy bears, each of which had different coloured noses.

In 1954, as a result of ever-increasing strikes and the red tape involved in running a business, Beer decided to retire and so the Invicta company closed.

SMALL INVICTA BEAR

This little bear, c.1938, has a wide, rather flat head. His light brown bulbous nose was created by pinching the fabric together and overstitching it tightly. His short arms curve upwards and the short chubby legs narrow at the ankle towards the large oval feet that do not have any claw stitching. Notice that the rexine on the paw pads has worn away to reveal the cotton backing underneath. Ht 33cm (13in), £300–400 ($450–600)

IDENTIFYING FEATURES

Large, clear-glass eyes were used on most bears, glued in on long wires.

The oblong, bulbous nose is made up of light-coloured vertical stitching.

A typical large paw with five claws stitched over onto the paw pad.

JOPI

HOW TO RECOGNIZE A JOPI BEAR

• Early bears are fully jointed, made of luxuriant mohair and are often coloured with dual plush.

• All Jopi bears have large glass eyes set close together, black silk nose stitching and large round ears that are set high on the head, above the prominent unshaved muzzle.

• Many Jopi bears have musical movements inside them, worked by bellows that are activated by pressing their tummies.

• Jopi bears have large heads stuffed with wood wool, while the bodies are stuffed with kapok.

• The remains of a stitch can often be found on the chest of a Jopi bear. This indicates where the paper label was attached, along with a brass bell.

• The bears have three stitched claws on their paws and feet, and felt paw pads.

Josef Pitrmann opened a factory making plush animals in 1910, but there are no further details on the history of his company until 1921. At that time he acquired a legally protected trademark, which took the form of an arch enclosing a representation of the skyline of Nuremberg. On the arch sat a bear holding a Christmas tree and a small panel with the word Jopi written on it. This was the first label that was used on early bears from 1922. Josef Pitrmann died in 1938, leaving his wife Marie and daughter Hilde to carry on the business, which they did successfully for many years. The last time details of the company were recorded was when it exhibited at the Nuremberg toy fair in 1959. Jopi bears were always of very high quality and are much prized today by collectors.

DUAL PLUSH BEAR
This bear has wonderful orange dual plush mohair. His large cupped ears are sewn across the facial seams. He has a prominent unshaved muzzle and is stuffed with kapok and wood wool. His body is rather flat, having no hump, and his feet are long and narrow. Each of his paws has three black stitched claws. This bear probably dates from 1925 and, unlike many other Josef Pitrmann bears, has no musical movement.
Ht 58cm (23in), £1,800–2,000 ($2,700–3,000)

MUSICAL DUAL PLUSH BEAR
This 1930 bear also has dual plush that is very thick and of high quality. His ears are set a little closer together than some of the other designs shown here, and his glass eyes are not quite as large. He has a musical movement, activated by pressing the bellows situated in his tummy. His unshaved muzzle has a black silk stitched nose and his foot and paw pads are made of felt. **Ht 46cm (18in), £1,800–2,000 ($2,700–3,000)**

JOPI RABBIT
This rare 1950 Jopi rabbit is in mint condition, retaining two paper labels and his brass bell, which is stitched to his chest. He is made in synthetic plush, his ears are wired so they stand upright, he has amber and black glass eyes and his nose is horizontally stitched in red, edged with black silk. He has three red stitched claws on his paws and feet, and his blue silk ribbon is the original one. **Ht 33cm (13in), £600–800 ($900–1,200)**

IDENTIFYING JOPI TOYS

Although many bears were being produced in the early years of the 20th century in the toy manufacturing areas of Germany, many of these are unrecorded. There are very few photographs or copies of company catalogues and advertisements that would help collectors to identify these bears – except of course if they were made by the larger makers such as Schuco, Steiff or Bing, which did keep more comprehensive records.

Jopi, however, is an exception to other smaller companies. There is a surviving page of a supplement to the main catalogue of 1934, showing some of the range of Jopi bears and other animals. There are also advertisements and, unlike some of the other manufacturers, Josef Pitrmann put labels on his bears. Some bears have even survived with their labels intact today.

In the mid-1920s the Jopi label changed. The word Jopi was shaped into a horse and rider with a whip until 1931; then a label with a stylized horse and a rider was used, with the word Jopi underneath.

On the existing page from the 1934 supplement it is possible to see some of the bears and animals that were being produced by Jopi at that time. There are two bear children called Mischka – one version is a baby bear with a bib and the other is a boy bear with a trumpet and an apron. These bears were only made in small sizes of 20–30cm (8–12in). There was also a larger bear called Jackie that was available in four different versions. The last known Jopi bears date from the late 1950s.

IDENTIFYING FEATURES

This Jopi card label is from the 1950s. It is unusual to find these labels intact.

This black silk nose is vertically stitched and is found on larger bears only.

This label, with its stylized horse and rider, was used from the 1930s to 1950s.

RED MOHAIR BEARS
These two bears, c.1930, are made in wonderful tipped red mohair, which is highly prized by collectors because of its rarity. They are also remarkably unfaded. The glass eyes are big, giving them expressive faces. Both bears have horizontal nose stitching. **Left: ht 33cm (13in). Right: ht 30cm (12in). £1,500–2,000 ($2,250–3,000) each**

APRICOT BEAR
This bear, c.1930, is of a light apricot colour with frosted tips. For many years Jopi bears like this one were wrongly attributed to Helvetic because the musical boxes inside them were stamped Helvetic. However, since the discovery of a Jopi catalogue it is now known that these bears were definitely made in Nuremberg by Josef Pitrmann. **Ht 38cm (15in), £1,500–2,000 ($2,250–3,000)**

MERRYTHOUGHT

The Merrythought toy factory was established in 1930 at Coalbrookdale, near Ironbridge in Shropshire, by W.G. Holmes and H.G. Laxton. The two men had become partners in 1919 when they opened a spinning mill in Yorkshire, making mohair yarn from raw mohair imported from South Africa and Turkey. They decided to open a toy factory, using their mohair yarn to make the toys. C.J. Rendell, head of production at Chad Valley Toys, was hired and he brought with him other skilled workers including the designer Florence Attwood, who was responsible for designing most Merrythought toys until 1949, and H.C. Janisch, head of sales at J.K. Farnell. Holmes and Laxton began production in rented space and when that was outgrown they moved in 1931 to a factory on the banks of the River Severn. The company was very successful from the beginning and after its first trade fair in Manchester it had so many orders that it was forced to move to much larger premises and increase its workforce. This same building is still in use today.

BINGIE BEAR
This c.1930 bear is designed with fixed legs but his arms and head are jointed. His cupped ears, lined with white artificial silk, are set on the side of his head. He has a centre seam running down his face and his dark brown eyes are made of glass and set wide apart. His arms are short, with oval felt pads with three long stitched claws, and his feet are extra large. The label is sewn on the inside of his leg. **Ht 66cm (26in), £300–600 ($450–900)**

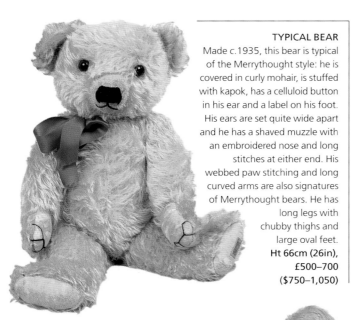

PRE-WORLD WAR II

The first Merrythought bears were produced in 1930. One of the earliest models, the Magnet bear, was first seen in the 1931 catalogue. Made in gold or coloured mohair, he was soft stuffed with a long nose and came in four sizes. Also in the 1931 catalogue was the original Merrythought bear: this bear came in ten different sizes in gold mohair and various colours of art silk, described in 1932 as the colour selection of the Paris dress designers. He was joined by a second Merrythought bear in long curly mohair plush who was dubbed an "aristocrat among bears". In these early days most of the work was done by hand, the only machines being a sewing machine and one for cutting out pads. All the finishing and the embroidery on paws, mouths and noses was done by hand, as it is still done today.

The Bingie bear first appeared in these early catalogues. This was a sitting bear cub made in five sizes and described as cuddly and winsome. A similar bear cub was made and christened Tumpy. Alongside these bears, a wide variety of animals were produced including Merrythought's famous monkey, with its expressive moulded face, designed by the artist Lawson Wood. There were novelties such as a laughing baby bear cub that could stand or sit and had an open mouth, and a Cutie Bingie described as a moving toy with jointed legs that could be placed in many positions. In 1933 more Bingies were introduced, starting with a dressed boy and girl and followed by a guardsman, a sailor and a ski girl. In 1939 a panda was born at London Zoo and Merrythought produced a special catalogue of pandas to celebrate the new arrival (see pp.116–17).

The 1930s were very busy and successful years for Merrythought. The factory was the largest soft toy company in England and in 1935 it expanded again, with orders flooding in. However, the situation changed in 1939 with the coming of World War II, when the British Admiralty took over the factory for map making. The company moved to temporary premises in Wellington, Shropshire, where it made fabric items such as sleeve badges, gas mask bags and covers for hot-water bottles to help with the war effort.

IDENTIFYING FEATURES

This celluloid button with the wishbone logo is from the 1930s. "Merrythought" is the Old English word for wishbone.

One of the earliest Merrythought embroidered foot labels, c.1930, this omits the word "hygienic".

From 1947 a card label such as this was hung from a ribbon tied around the neck of each Merrythought bear.

This label was in use from the 1930s until 1957 when "Hygienic Toys" was replaced by "Ironbridge Shrops".

MERRYTHOUGHT

DUTCH BEAR
The Dutch bear was introduced in 1938 and was made in eight sizes. This example is in mint condition. His distinctive characteristics include wide corduroy trousers with pockets and felt paw pads with three long claw stitches sewn right over the pad. His body, head and feet are made in alpaca, his eyes are glass and his nose and claw stitching is made of light brown silk. Another Merrythought Dutch bear was being produced at the same time, which had a velvet body and a head made of mohair. **Ht 30cm (12in), £200–300 ($300–450)**

"HYGIENIC TOYS"
These two Merrythought bears are made in pale gold mohair and both have the printed label with "Hygienic toys" written on it, which dates them to just after World War II. Their eyes are made of glass and their paw pads are cotton. The webbed stitching on their paws is very similar to that found on early Farnell bears, which is probably due to the influence of H.C. Janisch – a director of Merrythought who once worked for Farnell.
Left: ht 33cm (13in), £250–350 ($375–525). Right: 53cm (21in), £450–650 ($675–975)

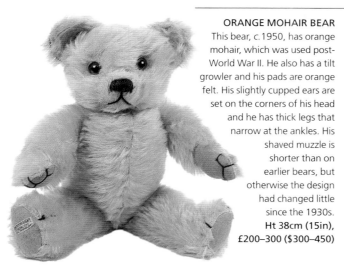

ORANGE MOHAIR BEAR

This bear, c.1950, has orange mohair, which was used post-World War II. He also has a tilt growler and his pads are orange felt. His slightly cupped ears are set on the corners of his head and he has thick legs that narrow at the ankles. His shaved muzzle is shorter than on earlier bears, but otherwise the design had changed little since the 1930s. **Ht 38cm (15in), £200–300 ($300–450)**

BLUE BEAR

This rare Merrythought is made in blue mohair. Such coloured bears were very popular in the 1930s when they were first made. When they left the factory they would have had a card label attached to the chest, but none of these have survived today. This bear's ears are cupped and he has large amber and black glass eyes set wide apart. **Ht 38cm (15in), £500–700 ($750–1,150)**

WINNIE-THE-POOH

Dated c.1976, this bear is made of mohair, is fully jointed and is one of the many Walt Disney characters that Merrythought produced between 1953 and 1980. Originally this bear would have been dressed in a red felt jacket that had "Pooh" written on it. Winnie-the-Pooh first appeared in the 1966 Merrythought catalogue, along with his friends Eeyore, Piglet, Kanga, Roo and Rabbit. **Ht 36cm (14in), £250–450 ($375–675)**

POST WORLD WAR II

In 1946 production started again at the factory on the River Severn under the management of B. Trayton Holmes, the son of one of the founders. However, in that same year the River Severn suffered severe flooding and many of the old samples were lost; the current production was severely cut as a result. But, even after this setback, by the following year a large volume of toys were again being manufactured to cope with increasing orders, and many of these were for the export market.

After World War II materials were very scarce, but Merrythought managed to continue production. In 1947 a catalogue was printed that featured some of the pre-war bears that were known as the "M" bears. These were kapok filled and fully jointed. Another design used at this time was the Print teddy. Only the head was made of mohair while the rest of his body was printed fabric, in order to economize on mohair. An automatic stuffing machine was shipped over from America in 1955, which increased output but this did not entirely replace the hand stuffing, which continues to this day.

The original designer, Florence Attwood, died in 1949. Over the next few decades various designers were employed until Jacqueline Revitt joined the company in 1970. Except for one brief interlude, she designed continually for Merrythought and is still doing so today.

From 1954 until 1980 many Disney cartoon characters, such as the Lady and the Tramp and Bambi were made by Merrythought. One of the most popular was Winnie-the-Pooh; his friends Kanga, Roo, Eeyore, Piglet and Rabbit also appeared in various versions.

In 1963 the Merrythought teddy bear of 1931 was redesigned with an unshaved muzzle and a flatter head. Initially the traditional bear was made in mohair, was fully jointed and kapok stuffed, but in 1971 synthetic plush was used for the first time.

From 1982 Merrythought's limited edition bears, all signed by Merrythought's chairman, B.T. Holmes, were sold in the USA by Tide River Inc. in direct response to the growing collectors' market in the States. In 1990 there was a special limited-edition Diamond Jubilee bear available to all Merrythought collectors, which was a huge success. Merrythought continues to make high-quality teddy bears for collectors all over the world today (see p.97).

IDENTIFYING FEATURES

This label has the words "Registered design" on it, which were often used for the first year or two that a design was manufactured.

This bulbous nose from the Winnie-the-Pooh bear is made of black silk and has vertical stitching.

MERRYTHOUGHT

IDENTIFYING FEATURES

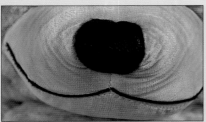

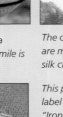

The Cheeky nose is stitched tightly over a protruding velvet muzzle and the wide smile is formed by two long stitches in black silk.

The circular paw pads on Cheekys are made in felt and have five black silk claws stitched over the seams.

This printed woven label has the words "Ironbridge Shrops" on it, which replaced "Hygienic Toys" from 1957. This wording was then used on all bears' labels until 1991.

MRS TWISTY CHEEKY

Mr and Mrs Twisty Cheeky were fitted with an internal frame that could be twisted into different positions. They formed part of a range of posable dressed standing toys. This early example is from 1966. Only the head is made in mohair while the body is covered in turquoise cloth and the paws in white fabric, with separated thumbs.
The red skirt and white pinafore are removable on Mrs Twisty, as are the dungarees, tie and collar on Mr Twisty. **Ht 28cm (11in), £500–700 ($750–1,050)**

COLOURED CHEEKY

This rare, faded blue art silk Cheeky was only made for a few years. This example is from 1959, and by 1960 pastel art silk was discontinued in favour of the brighter, newer nylon plushes. Coloured Cheekys are desirable today and fetch high prices. This one has pale pink ear linings and felt paw pads. His foot pads are made in art silk. **Ht 64cm (25in), £800–1,500 ($1,200–2,250)**

PUNKINHEAD

Punkinhead was made in three sizes for Eatons department store in Canada. With his white mohair topknot and black and white glass eyes, he was a fore-runner to the Cheeky bear. This one is a typical example from 1950. His body is brown mohair, apart from the gold mohair chest and ear linings, and he is fully jointed. His feet are made of velvet with felt pads and his felt shorts are sewn on. **Ht 41cm (16in), £2,000–2,500 ($3,000–3,750)**

EARLY CHEEKY

This Cheeky is an early example from 1960. He is made in art silk plush golden mohair, although a longer shaggy pile was also available at this time. Cheeky bears were very popular when they were first made and have remained so right up until today. This bear has glass eyes and large flat ears set on the side of his head with bells sewn in them. These early bears often have a label with the words "Registered design" on one foot. **Ht 38cm (15in), £350–500 ($525–750)**

SYNTHETIC PLUSH CHEEKY

This mid-1970s Cheeky is made in synthetic simulated mink plush. This type was made for about ten years and was available in four sizes. He has brown linings to his ears and a velvet muzzle with a black stitched nose and glass eyes. His brown felt circular paw pads have five claws stitched across the seams and his foot pads are made of brushed cotton. Ht 46cm (18in), £200–300 ($300–450)

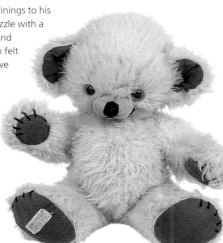

THREE GOLDEN CHEEKYS

These three 1965 Cheekys are made in London gold mohair. It is interesting to note the use of different colours and fabrics on the pads; collectors often think that they have been replaced but it is a characteristic of Cheeky bears to have such differences. In these examples the paws are felt and the feet brushed cotton. They also have locked-in plastic safety eyes, which were also used in later Cheekys. Front two: ht 38cm (15in). Back: 33cm (13in). £300–500 ($450–750) each

"CHEEKY" BEARS

One of the most popular Merrythought bears, Cheeky first made his appearance in 1956 at a trade fair. A customer picked him up and said "what a cheeky little bear" – the name stuck and he has been called Cheeky ever since!

Cheeky was designed by Jean Barber. His large round head and velvet muzzle makes him a very distinctive bear. He was originally made in one of two material combinations – gold plush and shaggy gold mohair, or art silk plush. Those first bears were kapok stuffed and had bells in their ears. In the following years many new versions of the bear appeared: in 1960 nylon plush was first seen and in 1962 an open-mouthed Cheeky appeared. Cheekys with musical boxes in them were made, as well as Cheeky muffs (*see* p.88), nightdress cases and even glove puppets. Mr and Mrs Twisty Cheeky arrived in 1966 – these were dressed bears with mohair heads (*see* opposite).

Cheekys continued to be made in a variety of fabrics over the next few years. Cheekys made in dark mink plush were created in 1970 and the bedtime bear with removable pyjamas and dressing gown carrying a hot-water bottle appeared in 1977. In the 1980s a very unusual luxury Cheeky appeared in thick, champagne-coloured plush. Instead of a velvet muzzle, he had a light brown fur muzzle that gave his face a very different expression.

Cheekys are just as loved today as they have ever been, and continue to offer the design and quality for which Merrythought is justly famous. Extremely sought after by collectors, they can fetch high prices.

PEDIGREE

HOW TO RECOGNIZE PEDIGREE BEARS FROM THE 1950s AND '60s

• They are fully jointed, made of mohair, stuffed with wood wool and kapok, and most have squeakers in their tummies.

• Some of the bears have labels with "Made in England" on them. This dates them from before 1955, as production then moved to Northern Ireland.

• Noses vary – they may be stitched in black silk, be made of moulded plastic or consist of a piece of stiffened black felt.

• Feet are small, legs straight and paw pads round. There is no claw stitching.

• They have a distinctive inverted T-shaped mouth embroidered in black silk. Eyes are often amber and black plastic but blue glass eyes were used on the later novelty bears.

• Some bears have bells in their ears and musical movements in their tummies.

In the mid-19th century two brothers, George and Joseph Lines, formed G.J. Lines Ltd. They manufactured baby carriages, wooden horses and other toys with great success. After World War I their three sons continued with the business, and purchased a factory in the Old Kent Road, London, which was when Lines Brothers was founded. They began to make soft toys and also registered another trademark, Triang Toys. They expanded into a further factory in 1924, at Merton in south-west London, and became the Triang Works. There they produced metal and wooden toys as well as prams, rocking horses and nursery furniture. The factory at Merton covered 27 acres and made Lines Brothers the largest toy company in the world. In 1931 the name Pedigree was registered as a subsidiary company and was first used by the Lines Brothers to advertise Pedigree prams. Pedigree Soft Toys was then formed and its first soft toys catalogue was produced in 1937.

MUSICAL & LARGE PEDIGREES
Both of these bears are c.1960. The bear on the left is a Musical Pedigree. He is fully jointed and made in thick mohair. His rather small oval nose is vertically stitched in black silk and he has a key-wind musical movement in his tummy. The unusually large bear on the right has very thick mohair. He has large, flat, soft ears and wide-apart eyes set on a dark brown felt backing.
Left: ht 41cm (16in), £250–350 ($375–525).
Right: ht 69cm (27in), £350–450 ($525–675)

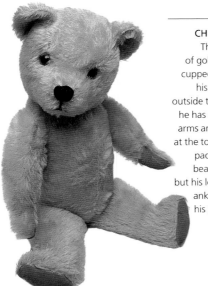

CHUBBY PEDIGREE BEAR

This bear, c.1950, is made of gold mohair and has small, cupped ears set at an angle on his head. His eyes are sewn outside the two facial seams and he has a round fabric nose. His arms are short and quite plump at the top, tapering down to the pads. Unlike some Pedigree bears he has chubby thighs, but his legs thin out towards the ankles. His feet are oval and his pads are made of velvet.
Ht 46cm (18in), £250–350 ($375–525)

POST-WORLD WAR II

In 1946 Countess Granville, the wife of the governor of Northern Ireland, was invited to open a new factory at Castlereagh Road, Belfast, Northern Ireland. Eventually most of Pedigree's toys and bears were made there. In 1946 Lines Brothers also purchased Joy Toys Ltd., whose factory was on the North Island of New Zealand. Over the next few years Lines Brothers continued to open factories in Canada, Australia, New Zealand and South Africa. Their toys, bears and famous plastic Pedigree dolls were selling in large numbers worldwide.

In 1955 all production of the company's soft toys was moved to Belfast and business boomed. During this time the factory was producing 400–500 jointed mohair bears a day, as well as the unjointed ones and a range of other toys. Pedigree toys were always of high quality and great care was taken to check for any faults in the stitching or material. Fifty machinists worked on sewing the bears together once five large cutting presses had cut out all the pieces. The heads and bodies were hand stuffed with wood wool while the arms and legs were machine filled. The bears were all hand finished and a team of around 50 specialist workers produced all the embroidery work on the noses.

New synthetic and washable fabrics became popular, as with all makers, from the 1960s onwards and the stuffing that was often used at this time was foam rubber. In 1966 a reorganization of the Lines Brothers companies took place and they became Rovex Triang. However, in 1971 the Belfast factory shut down and Rovex Traing collapsed. Pedigree moved the production of their soft toys to Canterbury, where they traded until operations closed down in 1988.

TWO POST-WAR BEARS

The bear on the left is c.1955 and he has two facial seams that make his muzzle protrude. He has the typical inverted T-mouth and a plastic nose. The other bear is c.1960. He has larger, soft ears and his mohair is very thick. Bears like this one often have bells in their ears. **Left: ht 50cm (20in), £200–300 ($300–450). Right: ht 56cm (22in), £250–350 ($375–525)**

IDENTIFYING FEATURES

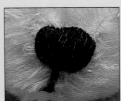

This label was used after the entire production of soft toys moved to Belfast.

These round felt noses were glued on but have sometimes been lost.

Moulded plastic noses were used from the mid-1950s onwards.

TYPICAL 1950s PEDIGREE

This is a typical Pedigree bear from the mid-1950s. He has a centre seam down his face and a horizontal seam across his head. His ears have the inner edge folded over and are sewn into the head seam – this is a characteristic of bears from the early 1950s. His legs are straight, with no definition at the ankles, his feet are round and his arms are short and straight with pointed paw pads. **Ht 46cm (18in), £250–350 ($375–525)**

NYLON PLUSH PEDIGREE

This 1960s bear is made in nylon plush and has glass eyes. The inset muzzle and red tongue were new innovations introduced in the 1960s by the designer Ann Wood, who had previously worked for Dean's. The bear has a "Made in Ireland" label on his back and a musical box in his tummy. **Ht 46cm (18in), £80–150 ($120–225)**

SCHUCO

HOW TO RECOGNIZE SCHUCO BEARS

• Early bears, c.1920, with the Yes/No mechanism had short mohair and black button eyes. Mohair bears on metal wheels made later in the 1920s also had a Yes/No mechanism.

• Early key-wind walking bears, dressed as soldiers in felt clothes, were similar to those made by Gebrüder Bing.

• Bears, animals, dwarfs wearing spectacles and monkeys in felt clothes were very popular in the 1920s.

• Fully jointed bears, c.1925, were made in bright mohair. They often had large glass eyes set close together on a wide head and vertical nose stitching.

• Baby bears from the 1930s had open mouths and red tongues. These usually came dressed in felt and cotton clothes, although there were some examples that came undressed.

• From the 1950s Tricky Yes/No bears were introduced, as well as a range of animals, pandas and dressed bears. Tricky bears have downturned paws with flat feet, and their muzzles are often shaved.

Heinrich Müller and Heinrich Schreyer founded the firm Schreyer and Co. in Nuremberg, Germany, in 1912. Müller had been employed by Gerbrüder Bing and Schreyer was a former furniture salesman from Nuremberg. In 1913 an early advertisement showed animals on wheels, mechanical tin toys, marching soldiers, clowns and other toy figures. With the advent of World War I the factory was closed; production started up again at the end of the war in 1918, but by then Schreyer had left the company because he thought there was no future in toy making. Müller was determined to succeed and began to look around for a new partner. Adolf Kahn joined him and together they started to expand the business. In 1919 a new factory was opened in Nuremberg and, in 1921, the trademark of Schuco, an abbreviation of the company's name, was registered.

YES/NO BEAR
This bear from 1925 has fabulously thick mohair and is in great condition. He has large ears set on top of his wide head, his eyes are glass and sewn inside the facial seams and he has a square, vertically stitched nose set on a pronounced muzzle. His body is chubby and lacks a hump, and his arms are straight with a slight curve at the paws. His paw pads are felt and he has plump, straight legs with well-defined ankles. **Ht 46cm (18in), £2,000–2,200 ($3,000–3,300)**

BELLHOP BEAR

Yes/No Bellhop bears are keenly sought after today. They were made in short gold mohair with sewn-on clothes that cannot be removed. This example is c.1923. His eyes are black shoe buttons – later Bellhop bears had glass eyes. His arms and legs are jointed and he has long, flat feet enabling him to stand freely. His condition is excellent, except for three recovered paw pads, and the fact that his card label is still intact adds to his value. **Ht 36cm (14in), £2,000–2,500 ($3,000–3,750)**

PRE-WORLD WAR II

Schuco produced a wide variety of novelty and mechanical bears, which were popular adult toys through the 1920s and '30s. The most enduring creation was the "Yes/No" bear, which first appeared at the Leipzig Fair in the spring of 1921 and was still being made when the firm was taken over in the 1970s. This bear nodded its head up and down and from side to side when the tail was moved as this activated a metal rod running through the length of the body connected to a ball-and-socket neck joint. The Yes/No bears were available in six sizes from 25cm (10in) to 61cm (24in) in short, long and extra long plush. The two larger sizes had tilt growlers and the smaller ones had squeakers. The company also made Yes/No bears and animals on wheels, with the words "Schuco-Patent" impressed on each wheel.

Diamanté eyes were an innovation of the 1920s, and could be fitted at extra cost to animals and bears; they were available in different colours, such as bright green, red and blue, and sparkled in the light. They were also used on the 1920s miniature Piccolo range (see pp.52–3).

In 1938, before the outbreak of World War II, Adolf Kahn left Germany to escape persecution and joined his son Eric in the USA. During the war the factory helped the war effort by making telephone equipment, and at the end of hostilities they turned to the production of kitchen hardware, continuing to produce just a few toys.

IDENTIFYING FEATURES

This eye of c.1925 is painted a reddish brown, which is characteristic of Schuco.

This mid-'20s nose has vertical stitching – earlier designs are horizontal.

The word "Schuco" was added to card labels on bears' chests in 1921.

LILAC-TIPPED BEAR

This lilac-tipped Yes/No bear's rare colour and wonderful condition makes him very desirable. Schuco used long-tipped mohair in a variety of bright colours such as green, purple and blue on their early bears and this one is c.1923. He is jointed and his Yes/No mechanism is activated by moving his tail. He would originally have had a paper label on his chest. **Ht 50cm (20in), £2,500–3,000 ($3,750–4,500)**

EARLY YES/NO BEAR

This Yes/No bear, c.1920, is made of short bright gold mohair. His eyes are black boot buttons, he has a black horizontally stitched nose, inverted Y-shaped mouth and small, cupped ears. He is hard stuffed and has quite small round feet with rayon pads. It is interesting to note that these early plain bears do not fetch the higher prices of later ones, which is unusual as early bears are normally worth more. **Ht 28cm (11in), £350–450 ($525–675)**

SCHUCO

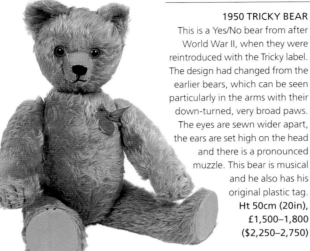

1950 TRICKY BEAR
This is a Yes/No bear from after World War II, when they were reintroduced with the Tricky label. The design had changed from the earlier bears, which can be seen particularly in the arms with their down-turned, very broad paws. The eyes are sewn wider apart, the ears are set high on the head and there is a pronounced muzzle. This bear is musical and he also has his original plastic tag.
Ht 50cm (20in),
£1,500–1,800
($2,250–2,750)

TRICKY DUTCH GIRL BEAR
This 1950s Dutch girl was one of a pair as she would originally have been sold with a Dutch boy. Such dressed bears only have mohair on the head, feet and paws; the body, which is clothed, is made of cotton. This is due to the fact that after World War II mohair was expensive and hard to find, so this design kept the cost down. These bears came in eight different colours. Another range had Tricky bears dressed as a Tyrolean couple. Ht 20cm (8in), £600–700 ($900–1,050)

PAIR OF TRICKY SIAMESE CATS
Dating from the 1950s, this pair of Siamese cats is in very good original condition. They are missing their plastic Tricky tags but would be a wonderful addition to any collection. Their bodies are cotton and they have the Yes/No mechanism. The straight legs and large oval feet lined with cardboard allow them to stand; the arms are also straight and have wide paws turning inward. It is unusual to find a pair of cats as they have often been split up. Ht 20cm (8in), £800–1,000 ($1,200–1,500) the pair

IDENTIFYING FEATURES

This large glass eye has a painted back and black pupil and is sewn on the facial seam.

This is an example of the short tail that was employed to act as a lever for the head movement found on Yes/No bears and animals.

TRICKY PANDA
This Tricky Panda, c.1953, has the same characteristics as the bears: straight arms with down-turned paws, large oval feet, a shaved muzzle and the Yes/No mechanism. In 1953 the Schuco Tricky range widened to include pandas, chimpanzees and monkeys, and the dwarfs that had been made before were continued. Tricky bears and other animals were made until 1960 when the soft-stuffed Heiga range replaced them. Ht 36cm (14in), £800–1,000 ($1,200–1,500)

IMMACULATE TRICKY BEAR

This fabulous Tricky Yes/No bear, c.1950, has thick curly mohair. He is in pristine condition and his plastic tag is still attached to the red ribbon on his chest. Because of his thick mohair he looks much more chubby than other bears and his face also has a different expression because of his unshaved muzzle. He is stuffed with wood wool; bears with soft kapok stuffing could be ordered as an alternative to this, and were available in four sizes. **Ht 50cm (20in), £1,500–2,000 ($2,250–3,000)**

POST-WORLD WAR II

In 1947 Adolf Kahn set up a branch of the Schuco Toy Company in the USA and imported Schuco products from Germany. In about 1949 Schreyer and Co. started full toy production again, with more new lines. In 1950 the Yes/No bear was reintroduced, this time with the famous "Tricky" label. A dressed Yes/No baby bear with an open mouth and a red felt tongue with round glass "googly" eyes was also made. A whole range of pandas, other animals and dwarfs were also included in this line, and the Piccolo series was reintroduced in slightly larger sizes.

In 1954 the Schuco "Rolly" clockwork bear appeared on roller-skates, holding a walking stick to balance him. This bear was very similar to the mechanical Bing design called the Skating Bear, which dates from 1912. Schuco also brought out the "Trip Trap" animals in the 1950s, which included a spaniel, poodle, kitten, fox terrier, dachshund and others. These were remarkably similar to the Gebrüder Bing designs – they were on rubber wheels, had leads and appeared to move on all fours quite naturally. The Tricky dwarfs that were made at this time had a centre seam down their felt face and shoe-button eyes, which means that they can be confused with the Steiff dwarf.

The Bigo Bello design was introduced in the 1960s, taking over from the Tricky bears. This new design included a range of fully posable bears. They carried labels bearing the Heiga logo, named after Mrs Herta Girtz who became director of production at this time.

Heinrich Müller died in 1958 and his only son, Werner, took over. However, by then the company was really struggling to fight off the competition from the Far East. They finally succumbed in the late 1970s when the company was sold to Dunbee Combex.

IDENTIFYING FEATURE

This is the Schuco Tricky plastic label. On the reverse side it says "Made in the US zone of Germany", which indicates it is pre-1953.

SCHUCO MINIATURES

Schuco is known for its jointed miniature bears, animals and characters, and in particular its Piccolo range. These were introduced in the early 1920s and were made until the 1970s. They came in several sizes – 6, 9 and 13cm (2½, 3½ and 5in) – and in a variety of colours. The bodies had an internal tinplate casing covered with mohair, which sometimes opened to reveal a cavity containing a manicure set, dice, a lipstick or even a compact. These charming miniature toys are very collectable today and the most highly sought after are those in bright, unusual colours and any novelty bears. In the 1920s and '30s they were fashionable adult accessories. For example, the perfume bottle bear could be put in a lady's handbag, and when the bear was brought out the head was removed to reveal the glass perfume bottle. Schuco produced a wide variety of Piccolo monkeys, many of which contain similar novelties to the bears, and some of which were mechanical. Other types of animals were also included. There were tiny bears with pins on the back, to be attached to a lapel and worn as a mascot.

JANUS BEAR
This Janus bear, c.1954, has two faces; a small brass knob situated at the base of the body can be turned to reveal either an ugly face (as shown) or a pretty teddy bear face. **Ht 9cm (3½in), £300–400 ($450–600)**

WIND-UP DANCER BEAR
This clockwork bear still has its original Schuco key from 1929 that, when wound up, makes him dance. He has a red felt cap with a tassel, his head, arms and body are made of mohair and he is only jointed at the head and arms. His feet are small and made of black metal. **Ht 13cm (5in), £800–900 ($1,200–1,350)**

NOVELTY BEARS
The two bears left and right are perfume bottles, c.1925 – their heads can be removed to reveal glass bottles. The bear on the right is particularly rare due to its burnt orange colour. The green roller bear, c.1930, is sitting in a friction-driven three wheeler tinplate car. Two versions of this design were made – this is the half bear version but there was also a removable 9cm (3½in) bear. Monkeys were also used instead of bears. **Left: ht 13cm (5in), £450–550 ($675–825). Centre: ht 9cm (3½in), £800–1,000 ($1,200–1,500). Right: ht 13cm (5in), £800–1,200 ($1,200–1,800)**

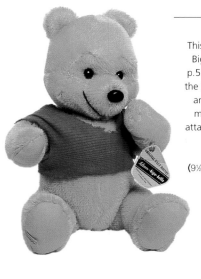

BIGO BELLO POOH BEAR
This bear, c.1965, is one of the Bigo Bello range of bears (*see* p.51). It is unjointed except for the head and has a plastic nose and glass eyes. He is made of mohair and has a paper label attached to him stating that he is the original Walt Disney Winnie the Pooh. **Ht 24cm (9½in), £150–200 ($225–300)**

SCOOTER BEAR
Dating from 1931, this scooter bear is made in gold mohair and is fully jointed. He is wearing a felt cap with a tassel and black felt trousers. The friction-action scooter is made of tinplate and has the Schuco logo stamped on one side. Other animals on scooters were made, such as monkeys and mice. **Ht 15cm (6in), £800–1,000 ($1,200–1,500)**

POWDER COMPACT BEAR
This pink mohair bear opens down the centre seam to reveal a tiny powder compact, a mirror and a powder puff. The brass neck also used to hold a lipstick. Such bears were popular fashion accessories by the time this bear was made in the late 1920s. **Ht 9cm (3½in), £400–500 ($600–750)**

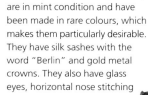

TWO YES/NO BERLIN BEARS
These two Yes/No bears, c.1968, are in mint condition and have been made in rare colours, which makes them particularly desirable. They have silk sashes with the word "Berlin" and gold metal crowns. They also have glass eyes, horizontal nose stitching and distinctive red felt tongues. The Yes/No head movement is activated by the tails. They were sold as souvenir items in transparent boxes. **Ht 13cm (5in), £500–600 ($750–900) each**

RARE MAUVE BEAR
This Schuco bear is made in brilliant mauve mohair. Many collectors try to find the whole range of colours, so this pristine example from 1930 would be extremely sought after due to its rare colour. He is fully jointed and has small black metal eyes, small ears stiffened with cardboard and a horizontally stitched nose. **Ht 9cm (3½in), £500–600 ($750–900)**

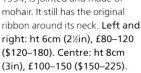

1950S BEARS AND RABBIT
The design of these two later bears from the 1950s has changed slightly from earlier examples as they have rounder faces and bodies. The rabbit, dating from 1954, is jointed and made of mohair. It still has the original ribbon around its neck. **Left and right: ht 6cm (2½in), £80–120 ($120–180). Centre: ht 8cm (3in), £100–150 ($150–225).**

STEIFF

HOW TO RECOGNIZE AN EARLY STEIFF BEAR

• Rod bears from 1904–5 are hard stuffed, have metal rod jointing and sealing wax noses. After 1905 bears were given stitched noses and claws in black silk.

• Early bears from 1905 have black boot-button eyes, long prominent shaved muzzles and cupped ears set on the corners of their wide heads. They are stuffed with wood wool and kapok.

• The bears are fully jointed, with very long arms reaching past the feet, and have curved paws and a distinctive hump on the back. Their legs are plump at the top, tapering to narrow ankles with felt pads. They should also have metal buttons in their left ears; many early bears have blank buttons.

• Squeaker-type voice boxes were used until 1908 when tilt growlers were introduced for the larger-sized bears.

Margarete Steiff was born in the small German village of Giengen-on-Brenz in 1847. As a child she was stricken by polio that left her paralysed and in a wheelchair. She studied needlework, even though it was difficult for her, and eventually learned how to use a sewing machine. In 1877 she opened a clothing shop for ladies and children and soon she was making a wide variety of garments. She had a good head for business and became very successful. Margarete had a wonderful imagination and would often tell stories to the local children. In 1880 she made her first felt toys in the form of elephant pincushions, which she gave to her nephews and nieces as gifts. Soon Margarete was making other animals such as camels, poodles, donkeys and monkeys, all of which proved very popular with her family and friends. Her brother Fritz felt her business could be expanded so he took a quantity of animals to the local market and sold them all. By the turn of the century the felt toy company was thriving, and Margarete's five nephews joined her in the business.

TWO ROD BEARS

These rod bears, c.1904, are very rare. They have metal rods connecting the joints and have very long arms and black button eyes. This type of bear typically has a horizontal seam running from ear to ear, a sealing wax nose and an elephant button in the ear. **Left: ht 50cm (20in). Right: ht 41cm (16in). Each bear: £12,000–15,000 ($18,000–22,500)**

BLANK BUTTON BEAR

This bear is an example of the next Steiff design, which was made between 1905 and 1906. He is stuffed with a lot of kapok and some wood wool and is very light. He has small black button eyes, cardboard disc joints held together with metal pinnings and apricot mohair. Early bears of this design have five stitched claws instead of four and a cone nose. **Ht 71cm (28in), £15,000–18,000 ($22,500–27,000)**

WHITE CENTRE-SEAM STEIFF
Dating from 1907, this very large bear is made in white mohair and has a centre seam down the middle of his face. Only every seventh bear had this feature because for bears of 41cm (16in) or more Steiff joined the bear fabric together, which enabled one extra head to be cut out of each length of cloth. **Ht 71cm (28in), £12,000–15,000 ($18,000–22,500)**

SMALL STEIFF BEAR
This bear is in mint condition. He is from 1907 and has a blank button in his ear and more wood wool stuffing than earlier designs, so he is not as heavy or soft. From 1905 to 1907 simple squeeze-type voice boxes were used. Tilt growlers were then introduced in 1908 for larger bears. **Ht 50cm (20in), £5,000–7,000 ($7,500–10,500)**

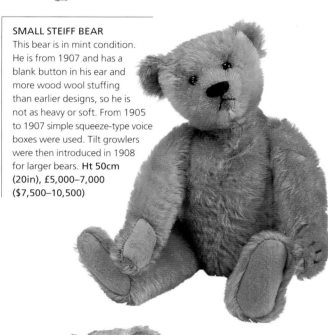

WHITE MUZZLE BEAR
Many novelty bears were introduced around 1908, including the muzzle bear. This is a very rare example, made in white mohair. These bears were made in 10 different sizes and were no doubt inspired by the many dancing bears that were a popular form of entertainment all over Europe. This particular bear has the printed Steiff button in his ear. **Ht 50cm (20in), £10,000–12,000 ($15,000–18,000)**

THE FIRST BEARS

One of Margarete's nephews, Richard, became a creative force in the company. He had studied art in Stuttgart and, while he was there, spent many hours at the Niles Animal Show drawing the performing bears. Richard designed mostly animals in the early years, until 1903 when he created the first teddy bear, inspired by the sketches he had made in Stuttgart. This bear was first shown at the Leipzig Toy Fair in 1903, and was known as Bar (bear) 55 PB. This was not the first toy bear Steiff had made, as bears had featured in catalogues since 1892. However, those earlier bears were not jointed but rigid, either standing upright or on all fours very like real bears. The new teddy bear was more like the jointed dolls that were being made in Germany at the time. It did not prove a success at the fair, and by the end of the day Richard had not taken a single order, until a buyer from an American toy company was entranced by it and ordered 3,000. There is not a single example of this bear known today, even in the Steiff museum.

Richard was not satisfied with the original design and decided to improve it, and in 1904 Bar 35 PB was introduced. This bear was made in mohair plush. The limbs were attached to the body with string, which was not entirely satisfactory as the joints became loose. Wire was tried as an alternative and then he finally settled on metal rods. The rod bears had metal buttons in their left ears with the Steiff trademark – an elephant with a S-shaped trunk stamped on it. Steiff tried to patent this button in 1904 but it was not allowed, so they patented the words "Button in the ear" instead.

Margarete was still not happy with the appearance of the bear and Richard finally came up with a new design in 1905, which had movable cardboard disc joints held together with metal pins. It was softer and rounder and had a much more appealing face. It proved to be very successful; in 1907 there was such a demand (nearly a million bears were produced) that it was known as the year of the bear.

IDENTIFYING FEATURES

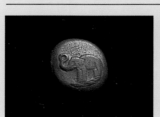

The elephant button was attached by two metal prongs to the left ear between 1904 and 1905.

This button was used between 1905 and 1950 and has the word Steiff printed on it. The white label was used from 1908.

The black stitched nose replaced the early sealing wax nose. Vertical stitching was used on larger bears only.

The prominent, long, shaved muzzle and cupped ears are typical features of early Steiff bears.

STEIFF

BLACK CENTRE-SEAM STEIFF

Black bears were made as a special order for England in 1912. The bears are sometimes called Titanic bears because England was mourning the sinking of the ship of the same name and the bears reflected the sombre mood of the country at this time. A distinctive feature shown here is the circle of red felt behind the black button eyes. Only a small number of black bears were made with a centre seam. The fabric became very fragile once it was dyed black, so few of these bears have survived. The hat and red bow on this bear are not original. Ht 50cm (20in), £15,000+ ($22,000+)

STEIFF NETTLE BEAR

This rare Steiff bear, c.1914, was made during World War I, when mohair was difficult to find. The fabric used here is a rough tweed type woven from the fibre of the nettle plant. Steiff produced a catalogue at this time showing a limited range of toys made in such substitute materials. For example, a pull-along bear on metal wheels was also made in this fabric. Ht 41cm (16in). £5,000–6,000 ($7,500–9,000)

PETSY BEAR

Blue glass googly eyes and large wired "posable" ears are the distinctive features of this bear from 1928. He has a centre seam running down his face, is soft stuffed and has long white mohair with brown tips. This type of bear was made in ten sizes up until 1930 and is very desirable today. **Ht 36cm (14in), £7,000–10,000 ($10,500–15,000)**

BROWN-TIPPED BEAR

This large mohair bear is in mint condition and, as such, is a very collectable example of a Steiff bear. He is c.1920 and has black and brown glass eyes sewn in on wire shanks. These eyes replaced the black buttons after World War I, although they had been available earlier for special orders only. He also has more kapok in his stuffing than earlier bears, making him softer and lighter and his body plumper. **Ht 71cm (28in), £10,000–12,000 ($15,000–18,000)**

GOLDEN BLONDE STEIFF

Dating from 1935, this bear is made in golden blonde mohair and has a button and tag in his ear. He has glass eyes and a shield-shaped vertically stitched nose. His ears are large, round and wide apart and he has long arms and a pronounced hump. He also has the final hand-sewn seam down the front of his body that is characteristic of Steiff bears. **Ht 64cm (25in), £7,500–8,500 ($11,250–12,750)**

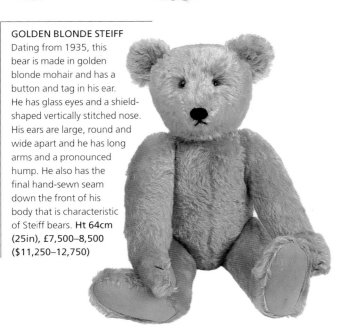

WORLD WAR I & BEYOND

Margarete Steiff died in 1909 but her motto, "Only the best is good enough for our children", was carried on by her brothers and nephews. The company grew but when World War I began it had a serious effect on the business as the Steiff brothers, Richard, Paul and Hugo, were called up to fight for their country. At this time the export business also ceased and output was severely reduced because much of the factory was turned over to war production.

Materials for making toys and bears were in short supply during the war as wool felt was used only for army uniforms. However, Steiff produced a range of bears directly after the war, in 1919, using paper plush. By 1920 business was getting back to normal. Manufacturing methods were modernized with the introduction of the conveyor belt system, which reduced costs and increased output. The company began to flourish again – new designs were introduced and much softer, lighter bears appeared, many in a new range of colours.

Novelty bears, such as Teddy Clown made from 1926 to 1928 and the smiling Teddy Baby from 1929, were a huge success, as were those with innovative movements, such as the Record series of toys. The years between the wars were a time of expansion and prosperity for Steiff.

WOOL PLUSH STEIFF BEAR

This bear is unusual because it is made in wool plush. This material has a very different look to mohair – rather than long and silky it is dull and bobbly. This fabric was also used on the Teddy Baby and the Dicky bear, which were being made around the same time. However, the material was not as well liked by customers as mohair. This bear's shape is typical of the 1930s (he is from 1935), with his long arms and large feet. **Ht 46cm (18in), £3,500–4,500 ($5,250–6,750)**

IDENTIFYING FEATURES

This Steiff button, with the underscored "F", was in use from 1905 until the 1950s. The yellow label underneath was used from 1934 to 1950.

This is the profile of a bear c.1930, which has a long, unshaved muzzle, black nose stitching and glass eyes.

STEIFF

CURLY BROWN STEIFF
The pristine condition of this wonderful bear, c.1930, adds significantly to his value. He has magnificent, thick, curly brown mohair and he is very large. His round ears are set wide apart and he has a very long, unshaved muzzle. His arms reach right down to his feet, which are large, and his ankles are narrow. He also has four claws sewn onto the plush of both his paws and feet. **Ht 71cm (28in), £10,000–12,000 ($15,000–18,000)**

1934 STEIFF BEAR
This bear is made in short gold mohair, which gives him a very different appearance to the more usual bears of this period that are made in longer mohair. In the 1970s this particular bear was sent by its owner to the Steiff factory for an appraisal. They confirmed that he was made in the 1930s but then attached a current 1970s chest tag to him. This is an example of extra identification being added to a bear long after it was made. This does happen a fair amount and can cause confusion, so you should be aware of this. **Ht 36cm (14in), £2,000–3,000 ($3,000–4,500)**

ORIGINAL TEDDY

This bear, c.1952, is an example of the modifications that were made to Steiff's initial teddy design after World War II. His paws are no longer curved, he has a shorter muzzle with a shield-shaped stitched nose and a rounder head with smaller ears set higher on the head than the previous design. His eyes are glass and he is stuffed with wood wool. **Ht 64cm (25in), £1,500–1,800 ($2,250–2,700)**

THE MASK BEAR

This new design was introduced in 1966, and this bear is probably an example from that very year. He has a distinctive, shaved, mask-shaped muzzle and his ears are set high on the head. He has no hump and his arms are longer and slightly curved, while his legs are short and stubby. The mohair is long and caramel coloured, synthetic stuffing has been used and the paw pads are made from Draylon. **Ht 30cm (12in), £200–300 ($300–450)**

TWO ZOTTY BEARS

These two Zotty bears from the 1970s follow a very distinctive design. They have open mouths lined with felt, and painted tongues. They also have bibs of peach-coloured mohair. Other manufacturers copied this design but only Steiff used the bibs. Left: ht 36cm (14in), £200–300 ($300–450). Right: 20cm (8in), £150–200 ($225–300)

POST-WORLD WAR II

After the devastation of World War II it was some years before production started again. A limited number of toys were then made for the occupying American troops and for export to the USA, and by 1950 there was a large Steiff display at the Nuremberg Toy Fair. However, there were criticisms of the old design of bears so a new look was called for. The realistic style of bear was changed to one with a rounder head, shorter arms and no hump. At this time the button was also changed and a blank button was used from 1948 to 1950. Many bears also had a white label marked "Made in the US zone" stitched into their side seam. A button with Steiff written in capital letters was used for a few years around 1950 and then in 1952 the button with Steiff in raised script came into use. This new button design was then employed right up until the 1970s.

In 1953 Steiff celebrated their 50th anniversary of the teddy bear by bringing out the "Jackie" and "Nimrod" bears. Jackie is a bear cub, with a unique nose design of a single pink horizontal stitch across the black nose stitching. The Nimrod bear was dressed as a hunter and carried a rifle. In the 1960s and '70s the demand was for softer bears with synthetic fillings. Steiff suffered, along with other companies at this time, from competition from Asia but by the beginning of the 1980s the teddy bear boom in the USA created renewed interest in Steiff. Antique Steiff bears began to be sold in auction in London and New York for high prices. The demand for Steiff was therefore stronger than ever and the company was able to prosper greatly once again. It is still a thriving business today (*see* p.99).

IDENTIFYING FEATURES

This is a typical ear from a 1930s bear. It is large and round and set wide on the head. Buttons were put in the left ears.

This chest tag from Original Teddy was in use from 1952 to 1972 and was also used on replica bears from 1983.

This tag is from the Zotty bear. It was used from 1972 and was stitched to the light-coloured bib on his chest.

This button has Steiff written in cursive script on it. Along with the yellow label, it was in use from 1952 to 1972.

TERRY'S

HOW TO RECOGNIZE A TERRY'S BEAR

The bears on this spread are of the type usually attributed to William Terry, with the following characteristics:

• Large cupped ears set high on the head and large clear glass eyes with big black pupils and painted backs.

• A triangular-shaped head and long narrow shaved muzzle that turns up at the end. The black nose stitching is either shield-shaped and vertical, or distinctive horizontal stitching set on top of the nose.

• Early bears prior to 1921 are hard stuffed with wood wool, fully jointed and made of mohair. Many have long straight bodies with the head set low into the shoulders and a high humped back. The large oval feet have cardboard inserts and felt or cotton twill pads.

• Some bears have webbed paw stitching similar to J.K. Farnell's and Merrythought's.

William J. Terry is one of England's oldest soft toy manufacturers, along with J.K. Farnell. It produced fur-covered animals, like Farnell, but it also used felt and plush. The company was first established in Stoke Newington, London, in 1890, and it was not until after 1909, when it opened a new factory at 25 Middleton Road, Hackney, that it started to make mohair bears. The German companies of Bing and Steiff had dominated the English teddy bear market for a few years, but when the first English teddy was made by J.K. Farnell around 1908 other English manufacturers began to follow suit. Terry's made its first mohair bears around 1912, but previously it had been famous for manufacturing a toy dog with a label reading "I am Caesar", modelled on a small terrier that had been King Edward VII's favourite dog. When the king died in May 1910, the dog followed the coffin in the funeral procession and made a lasting impression on the crowds thronging the route. Terry's company logo was a cut-out card label of a terrier dog based on Caesar, and its bears were marketed under the name "Terryer Toys".

LARGE HARD-STUFFED BEAR
This large bear, c.1915, has very high-quality gold mohair and he is hard stuffed with wood wool, making him heavy. It was not until 1920 that kapok was introduced to make the bears softer and lighter. He has large ears and glass eyes, which are typical of English bears of this period. Positive identification of Terry's bears is very difficult because their only labelling was a card swing tag that was easily lost or removed; the only clues, therefore, are old photos or advertisements in trade papers.
Ht 7cm (28in), £2,000–2,500
($3,000–3,750)

ORIGINAL-CONDITION BEAR

Dating from 1914, this bear was in original condition when he was purchased but he was very dirty and needed some restuffing and restoration. When he was opened up he was found to have large square washers on all his joints, which is unusual as most old bears have round washers. He has horsehair stuffing in his feet, his felt paw pads are lined with linen and his large ears have thick felt wadding in them. He also has a large tilt growler. **Ht 63.5 cm (25in),** £2,000–2,500 ($3,000–3,750)

SHAGGY-MOHAIR BEAR

This bear, c.1918, has all the characteristics associated with Terry's bears: shaggy mohair, a long straight body with a high pointed hump, large ears set high on his head, clear glass eyes with painted backs and a long shaved muzzle. His nose is square and vertically stitched, his feet are large and oval and he has long arms. **Ht 51cm (20in)** £1,200–1,500 ($1,800–2,250)

GOLDEN-MOHAIR BEAR

This bear, c.1915, also has the characteristics commonly attributed to William Terry: the ears are set high on the head, he has a triangular-shaped face with a shaved muzzle, and plump arms reaching to feet that are large and oval with cardboard inserts. His mohair, which came from mills in Yorkshire, is of the highest quality, and the design of this bear is typically English, rather than a copy of earlier German bears. **Ht 41cm (16in),** £1,000–1,200 ($1,500–1,800)

WAR-TIME BOOM

The English toy-making industry was thriving in 1912 and economically the country was experiencing a boom. When war was declared in 1914, a ban on German imports was enforced and English manufacturers like Terry's faced an unprecedented demand for the popular teddy bear. Skilled workers were at a premium and the company operated from another factory, the Welby Works in Lavender Grove, Hackney, which was extended in 1915 as the company prospered.

William Terry and other toy manufacturers attended the first British toy fair in 1915, which was very successful. This was quickly followed by an even larger exhibition organised by the Board of Trade to promote British products. As the war progressed the anti-German feeling became strong, reflected in the public demand for a bear with an all-British look. Terry's created a bear with a long straight body, plump arms and large clear glass eyes, but it is not always easy to identify a Terry's bear as the paper label is often lost. In 1921 Terry's introduced soft-stuffed kapok-filled bears under the trademark "Ahsolight".

William Terry died in 1924 and his son Frederick carried on the business, with his sales agent J. Hopkins, in showrooms in Aldergate Street, London. The company closed prior to World War II.

PRISTINE-CONDITION BEAR

This bear, c.1915, has long shaggy mohair in pristine condition. His large square nose, with longer central stitches reaching down to the mouth, is a design associated with William Terry. There is no webbed claw stitching on this particular bear; similar Terry's bears have been found that do have it, but often these are larger-sized bears. His arms are quite short and the paw pads are made of felt. **Ht 35.5cm (14in),** £800–1,200 ($1,200–1,800)

IDENTIFYING FEATURES

This nose has the Terry's horizontal stitching set on the top of the muzzle.

This is the large clear glass eye with its painted back and big black pupil.

This shows the typical Terry's profile: a low-set head, high hump and upturned muzzle.

WENDY BOSTON

HOW TO RECOGNIZE A WENDY BOSTON BEAR

• Most Wendy Boston bears are unjointed and have arms that curve upward. They also have short clipped muzzles and tightly bound, vertically stitched noses.

• Except for a few early bears, they are made of nylon plush and are filled with foam chippings. These chippings have sometimes disintegrated over time, leaving the bear flat.

• The bears have black and amber plastic locked-in safety eyes and their ears are cut all-in-one along with the head.

• They have straight, stocky legs with no ankles and the paws and pads have short nylon plush. Many of them also have sewn-in satinized labels attached to the paw or inside of the leg, or sometimes the labels are stitched onto their backs.

Wendy Boston founded her business with her husband Ken in 1945, making soft toys in a small shop in South Wales with a staff of just three. Wendy designed the bears and Ken was responsible for the marketing and management of the company. By 1947 they were employing 16 staff and had also begun to make a traditional range of animals as well as bears. Some of these animals were jointed and made in mohair. Toys were in short supply in England just after the war and soon the company was selling everything they could produce. They decided to expand, and opened a factory in Abergavenny in 1948, hiring a staff of 30. They realized at this point that they had to compete with other established toy companies by producing something original. Wendy, who was ahead of her time, was aware of the changing attitudes towards toys by safety-conscious parents. She therefore broke with tradition by designing a bear that was safe, hygienic and washable. This bear was to change the face of the soft toy market for ever.

GOLDEN BEAR
This 1959 bear has large ears, cut all-in-one with the head so that after washing it could be hung on the line to dry and wouldn't fall apart. He also has no joints in the arms, legs or neck so that the limbs couldn't be pulled off. These features indicate that the bear was designed with safety in mind at all times. **Ht 56cm (22in), £50–70 ($75–105)**

A REVOLUTIONARY IDEA

Wendy Boston began by inventing the locked-in plastic safety eye. She then developed her ideas further and in 1954 the first nylon-covered, foam-filled teddy bear was successfully test-marketed. This bear was filled with foam chippings and could be washed and even put through a mangle without losing its shape and softness. It was even tested by Hoover, who issued a certificate recommending a gentle wash and spin dry in their washing machines.

In 1960 the company changed its name to Wendy Boston Playsafe Toys Ltd. The advertisement actually stated: "We are the first firm in the world to make a complete range of washable, sponge-filled nylon soft toys with moulded, screw-locked eyes." Wendy Boston did also make a range of mohair bears – both jointed and unjointed – but these obviously did not carry a label advising washing!

Wendy Boston bears and soft toys were exported all over the world and it was claimed that she had 28 per cent of the whole market in 1964. However, all the wonderful, innovative safety features unfortunately added to the cost of production and so the company's profits began to decline as a result. It was found that similar soft toys could be made much more cheaply in the Far East. Soon toys from that area began to flood the world markets and so the demand for Wendy Boston bears dropped significantly. At the same time Wendy's health was failing and so, in 1968, she decided to sell the company to Denys Fisher Toys. It continued production until 1976, when the company finally closed down.

GOLLY AND BEAR
This 1962 bear is two-tone nylon plush and, typically, he holds his curved arms out sideways. Each paw has three stitched black claws.

The 1960 golly, with his white raised eyebrows, is also typical Wendy Boston. **Bear: ht: 53cm (21in), £40–50 ($60–75). Golly: ht 30cm (12in), £30–40 ($45–60)**

WHITE BEAR
This 1960 bear is made in white nylon plush. He has the safety locked-in plastic eyes that were invented by Wendy Boston. Each eye has a circle of amber plastic, a black bolt that forms the pupil and a nut holding it all together. **Ht 48cm (19in), £30–40 ($45–60)**

ADVERTISEMENTS
This is a compilation page, made up from Wendy Boston catalogues of the 1960s. The advert at the bottom shows some of the colours that the bears were available in, but they also came in pink and blue plush. On the top right is a certificate of washability that was issued by Hoover stating that Wendy Boston bears could be washed in washing machines. **£20–25 ($30–38)**

WENDY BOSTON PLAYSAFE TOYS

BASIL BRUSH
Basil Brush was a favourite British TV character and this 1972 version was made after the takeover by Denys Fisher in 1968. He is nylon plush and has an all-in-one head and ears. He also has an open mouth and his Wendy Boston label has been sewn into the side of his red trousers. **Ht 39.5cm (15½in), £40–60 ($60–90)**

IDENTIFYING FEATURE

Many Wendy Boston bears still retain their labels as they were stitched all around the edges to a foot, the inside of a leg or even the back of a bear. This 1959 label has "Washable in lukewarm suds" written on it.

OTHER MAKERS – ENGLISH

This red and white embroidered label is from a Peacock bear that was made c.1932. This was stitched onto a felt paw pad.

This is an embroidered blue and white label from an Ealon bear, c.1930, which has been sewn onto the felt paw pad.

World War I gave English soft toy makers a great opportunity to step into the gap created by the ban on German imports. The first British teddy bear, whose design was no doubt inspired by the German companies Steiff and Bing, is thought to have been made by J.K. Farnell as early as 1908. By 1914 there was such a huge demand for the teddy bear that many companies added teddies to their range. After the war was over the British soft toy industry continued to thrive and from the 1920s and '30s come some of the most collectable English bears. At the outset of World War II, however, production of bears was cut right back as factories concentrated on the war effort, and after the war it took a while for soft toy manufacturing to get started again. The design of the bear changed at this time – the faces were flatter and the arms and legs shorter in order to save mohair – but by the 1960s the market was changing and cheaper, washable synthetic bears became popular. Sadly, in the 1970s many of the leading soft toy makers went out of business.

HARWIN ALLIED BEAR
Harwin and Co. was established in north London in 1914 and continued in business up until 1930. Dorothy Harwin designed this bear, dressed as a British officer, around 1914, and he was part of a range of patriotic bears that were each dressed in the uniform of the Allied soliders. He is in excellent condition and is also very rare. **Ht 30cm (12in), £2,000–3,000 ($3,000–4,500)**

TWO STEEVANS BEARS
These bears, both c.1915, have metal chimes in their hard, barrel-shaped bodies. The Steevans factory they were made at was founded around 1908 and ceased production in 1920. **Left: ht 25cm (10in), £200–300 ($300–450). Right: ht 28cm (11in), £300–400 ($450–600)**

PEACOCK BEAR
This bear has large cupped ears and a shaved muzzle. His horizontal nose stitching is characteristic of Peacock bears. He was made after Chad Valley took over Peacock and Co. Ltd. in 1931 and moved them to east London. The Peacock range slowly disappeared and no bears with this label were made after 1939.
Ht 71cm (28in),
£1,200–1,500
($1,800–2,250)

PIXIE TOYS BEAR
Pixie Toys were founded in the early 1930s at Stourbridge, Worcestershire. They employed Elizabeth Simmond, a designer who had worked for Norah Wellings and Merrythought and, as a result, Pixie bears share some characteristics with bears from those two makers. This bear, c.1950, has the typical Pixie webbed stitching on his paws.
Ht 38cm (15in),
£200–300 ($300–450)

EALON TOYS BEAR
Suffragette Sylvia Pankhurst founded Ealon Toys in east London in 1914. They made high-quality soft toys and traded until the early 1950s. The bear shown here is from 1930; he is made of golden mohair, is fully jointed and has felt paw pads and glass eyes. **Ht 51cm (20in), £400–500 ($600–750)**

LEFRAY TOYS BEAR
Lefray Toys was established in 1948 in west London and after a few moves within and around London it relocated to Wales in 1969 and is still trading there today. This bear, made in the 1960s, has large flat ears, plastic eyes and is made in mohair. The nose is vertically stitched, his body is chubby and he has short arms and legs.
Ht 41cm (16in),
£200–300
($300–450)

TINKA-BELL
This 1952 bear is made of sheepskin, which is a material that was used after World War I when mohair was in short supply. Several different companies made these bears but this one was by Plummer Wandless & Co. They had a factory in Sussex and produced a large number of bears from 1946 until 1971.
Ht 46cm (18in),
£100–200
($150–300)

OTHER MAKERS – AMERICAN

When Clifford Berryman drew his very famous cartoon in *The Washington Post* in 1902, of President Theodore Roosevelt refusing to shoot a bear cub, it is thought to have inspired Rose and Morris Michtom to create their first toy bear. That bear proved to be a great success and they went on to establish the Ideal Novelty and Toy Company in New York in 1903. The bear soon became known as the Teddy Bear because of its association with the President, whose name was shortened to Teddy Roosevelt. Other manufacturers sprung up, quick to see the money-making possibilities. Many novelty bears became available, such as the Electric Eyes Teddy, the Strauss Whistling Bear and the Laughing Roosevelt Bear. A lot of the famous manufacturers were centred around New York but many vintage American bears remain unidentified today – they are only recognizable by their typical features, such as shoe-button eyes set close together, horizontally stitched noses, low-set rounded ears, heads that are set down into their bodies and wood wool stuffing.

IDEAL BEARS

The two seated bears are typical early Ideal bears from 1907. They have triangular-shaped heads, black button eyes and large, black, vertically stitched noses. Their long narrow bodies are soft stuffed and they have pointed felt paw pads. The Ideal bear at the back, c.1910, is wearing an original Teddy Roosevelt Rough Rider outfit (*see* p.77). His head, feet and paws are mohair. **Left:** ht 33cm (13in), £700–800 ($1,050–1,200). **Centre:** ht 41cm (16in), £2,000–2,500 ($3,000–3,750). **Right:** ht 30cm (12in), £800–900 ($1,200–1,350)

B.M.C. BEAR

The New York-based Bruin Manufacturing Co. (B.M.C.) only produced bears between 1907 and 1909, so they are extremely rare today. This bear, c.1907, is made of high-quality, long, silky mohair. He is stuffed with wood wool and kapok and so is very soft and light. His head is triangular shaped and he has a distinctive, pointed muzzle. Such B.M.C. bears can often still be found with their labels intact, which is unusual for such early examples. **Ht 36cm (14in), £3,000–4,000 ($4,500–6,000)**

COLOMBIA MFG CO. ROOSEVELT BEAR

This long-bodied, fully jointed bear of 1907 is made in short gold mohair. He has glass eyes and a composition open mouth with glass teeth. When his tummy is squeezed the mouth opens to make him laugh. His paw pads have been made using rather poor-quality felt. **Ht 46cm (18in), £2,000–2,500 ($3,000–3,750)**

AETNA BEAR

This bear, c.1910, is made in pale gold mohair and has glass eyes and feet that are slightly pointed and lined with cardboard. Stamped on his foot is the word Aetna, set in an oval, although this is often faded. The Aetna Toy Animal Co. produced its first bears around 1907. **Ht 36cm (14in), £2,000–2,500 ($3,000–3,750)**

LAUGHING ROOSEVELT

Dating from 1908 this rare Roosevelt bear differs from the one made by the Columbia Mfg Co., as the mohair is of higher quality and the teeth are moulded plaster. The mouth is opened and closed by pulling a ring on the back of the neck, which pulls the chin downward. His eyes are made of glass and the ears were gathered together and sewn on the side of his head. **Ht 48cm (19in), £2,000–2,500 ($3,000–3,750)**

IDENTIFYING FEATURES

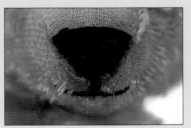

This is typical nose stitching from an Ideal bear of 1907 – it is large and stitched horizontally on top of the muzzle.

This profile is very characteristic of an early Ideal bear as the muzzle is very long, sloping and shaved.

OTHER MAKERS – AMERICAN

HECLA BEAR

Hecla set themselves up in direct competition to Steiff, so their bears look very similar to those by the German company. Hecla was short-lived, only making bears for a few years in the early 1900s during the boom years of the teddy bear. They used imported German mohair and this very large bear from 1908 also has the characteristic rust-coloured mouth, nose and claw stitching. His eyes are glass and set close together, the arms and legs are long and he has a pronounced hump. **Ht 76cm (30in), £6,000–7,000 ($9,000–10,500)**

BEAR DOLL

Novelty bear dolls with the mohair body of a teddy bear and the face of a doll appeared c.1908. The faces were imported from Germany and were either made of composition, bisque or celluloid. Harman, the New York Mfg. Co. and other US companies made them, but the maker of this example is unknown. He has a celluloid face, his body is made from mohair and he is fully jointed. Such bear dolls are very rare. **Ht 30cm (12in), £1,000–1,200 ($1,500–1,800)**

PATRIOTIC BEAR

The Art Novelty Co. was based in New York and in 1908 they claimed they were the originators of the patriotic red, white and blue plush bears. This particular example from that year is in mint condition. His body and head are rigid while the arms are jointed. The collar and sash are original and the colour of the mohair is still very bright. **Ht 41cm (16in), £1,200–1,500 ($1,800–2,250)**

RED ELECTRIC-EYE BEAR

Various manufacturers made electric-eye bears and, while some remain unidentified, the American Made Stuffed Toy Co. definitely produced this example from 1908, as there is a catalogue to prove it. His eyes are small light bulbs, activated by a switch, and the batteries are placed in his body through a seam at the back. **Ht 56cm (22in), £1,000–2,000 ($1,500–3,000)**

UNIDENTIFIED BEAR

This is a typical American bear made by an unidentified company during the years up to the 1920s. The gold mohair is short, the eyes are made of brown and black glass and the nose is narrow and horizontally stitched. This bear also has the characteristic football-shaped body, short, straight arms and legs and small feet with felt paw pads. **Ht 46cm (18in), £400–500 ($600–750)**

KNICKERBOCKER BEAR

The Knickerbocker Co. began making bears in the 1920s and traded right up until the 1980s. Dating from 1930, this bear is made in rich brown mohair and has a triangular head with very large round ears. The eyes are made of black and brown glass and are set wide apart on either side of the pointed muzzle, which has a square, vertically stitched nose at the end. His arms are set low on the shoulders and end in felt paw pads. **Ht 43cm (17in), £400–500 ($600–750)**

OTHER MAKERS – GERMAN

IDENTIFYING FEATURES

The German plush toy industry began around 1905 and was centred in the Sonneberg and Neustadt region. However, Steiff had already produced their first bears in 1903–4 in the town of Geingen 300km (200 miles) away. The Sonneberg and Neustadt area had been famous for toy and doll making since the 16th century and responded to the demand for teddy bears quickly. Most bears were made by cottage-industry workers and were destined for the American market but, at the same time, in the Nuremberg area there were 30 or more larger manufacturers including G.B.R. Bing, William Strunz, Schuco and Josef Pitrmann of Jopi. Production was slowed down by World War I but by the 1920s supply was back to normal. The design of the bears changed – there were more brightly coloured bears and lots of fashionable adult novelties. After World War II German manufacturers responded to the demand for a new style of teddy, and synthetic fabrics were introduced. However, with the development of the collectors' market in the 1980s many makers turned to producing the traditional bear again.

This is the felt-padded foot of a Strunz bear dating from 1908. Although it is similar to a Steiff foot it is not so slim.

Strunz six-sided metal buttons were placed in bears' ears. This one is from 1908 and has a white label with "Strunz Toys" written on it.

WILLIAM STRUNZ BEAR
This bear, from 1908, has black button eyes and cupped ears. His prominent muzzle has horizontal black silk stitching. He is made in mohair and has long arms and legs and felt paw pads with cardboard inserts. Like the larger bear on the right, he too looks like a Steiff bear. Ht 41cm (16in), £1,200–1,500 ($1,800–2,250)

STEIFF-LIKE STRUNZ BEAR
The bear of 1908 shown above is similar to a Steiff bear. Its maker, William Strunz of Nuremberg, put a metal button with a white label in its ear, which was again reminiscent of Steiff's own button. Needless to say, Steiff was almost in permanent litigation with Strunz, who had copied many of their designs. Ht 48cm (19in), £2,000–3,000 ($3,000–4,500)

BLONDE PETER BEAR
Made by Gebrüder Sussenguth, this blonde Peter bear, c.1925, is much rarer than the brown-tipped version below and he still retains his chest tag. He has unusual googly glass eyes that move from side to side in unison with his tongue, which is set in an open mouth with teeth, giving him a ferocious appearance. The nose is moulded black composition and the hollow head is made from pressed cardboard stapled together. **Ht 36cm (14in), £2,500–3,500 ($3,750–5,250)**

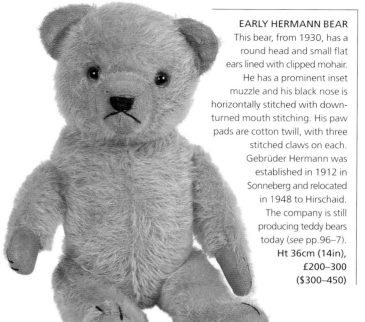

EARLY HERMANN BEAR
This bear, from 1930, has a round head and small flat ears lined with clipped mohair. He has a prominent inset muzzle and his black nose is horizontally stitched with down-turned mouth stitching. His paw pads are cotton twill, with three stitched claws on each. Gebrüder Hermann was established in 1912 in Sonneberg and relocated in 1948 to Hirschaid. The company is still producing teddy bears today (see pp.96–7). **Ht 36cm (14in), £200–300 ($300–450)**

BROWN-TIPPED PETER BEAR
These Sussenguth Peter bears are usually found in mint condition and often come with their original box, as shown here. The design was not very popular and did not stay in production for long. This one dates from 1925. **Ht 36cm (14in), £2,000–2,500 ($3,000–3,750)**

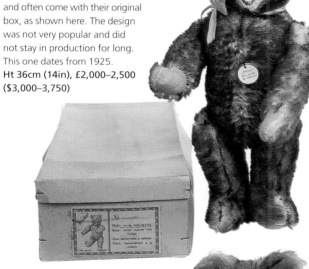

LATER COLLECTORS' BEAR
Made in high-quality golden mohair, this large Hermann bear, c.1985, is in pristine condition. He still has his red chest tag with the words "Hermann Teddy Original". His eyes are glass and the design of the head has changed from the the earlier bear, pictured above, as the muzzle is unshaven and the ears are larger. **Ht 71cm (28in), £300–400 ($450–600)**

NICKLE KNACKLE BEAR
This bear was made by Rudolf Haas, a little known teddy bear manufacturer who advertised its first bears in 1925. The Nickle Knackle bear first appeared in 1928. It incorporates an ingenious mechanism: when the left arm is moved up and down the bear nods and growls and when the right arm is moved the head turns from left to right. **Ht 36cm (14in), £2,500–3,000 ($3,750–4,500)**

OTHER MAKERS – FRENCH

This metal button has the words "Unis France" on it and was used by the French maker Marcelle Pintel around the 1930s.

During the late 19th century the famous French toy maker Roullet de Camp made mechanical performing bears covered with real fur. However, it was not until World War I, when German bears were no longer imported, that French manufacturers really started to make jointed plush bears. Marcelle Pintel was one of the first to do so – in 1920 it produced mohair bears. Thiennot, who had once worked for Pintel, was another early maker. He began producing bears in 1919 under the trade name Le Jouet Champenois. Fadap, who became one of the largest soft toy producers, was established in 1925. During World War II production slowed or stopped altogether at the factories. Some of the bears from this quieter period are made from strange fabrics, such as blanket material, and after the war cotton plush was used instead of mohair. During the 1950s fully jointed bears were popular, but by the 1970s Far Eastern toys had flooded the market and most of the factories closed down.

FADAP BEAR

This bear, c.1930, is made of cotton plush, which was a fabric used instead of mohair on its cheaper range of bears. He is also hard stuffed, which is a typical feature of French bears. Some of Fadap's bears still have the metal button and paper tag in their ears, although these are more often than not missing today. **Ht 58cm (23in), £300–400 ($450–600)**

UNIDENTIFIED FRENCH BEAR

French bears can be incredibly difficult to identify. This is because they were mostly made without labels and many of the designers moved from factory to factory, which means bears from different companies have similar appearances. This particular bear is by an unknown French maker and dates from 1935. **Ht 51cm (20in), £200–300 ($300–450)**

PINTEL MECHANICAL BEAR

Dating from c.1930, this rare bear has a clockwork mechanism that, when wound up, enables the bear to perform somersaults. He also has a collar around his neck with a round metal tag saying "Unis France", which was the trademark used by Pintel. The company also made another mechanical bear on a metal tricycle as early as 1915 – this was very well received and was made until 1940. **Ht 13cm (5in), £400–500 ($600–750)**

CRÉATION TIENOT BEAR

The downturned mouth of this bear, c.1960, is a notable feature of French bears. He has lost most of his fur, which is probably because some of the fabric that was used on him was not of the best quality. The company changed its name to "Création Tienot" in 1957 – before that it was known as Thiennot. **Ht 30cm (12in), £100–200 ($150–300)**

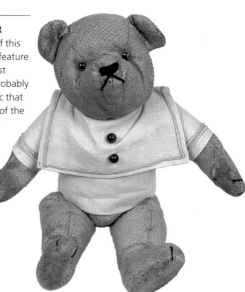

STANDING FRENCH BEAR

This unusual French bear was probably made by Fadap, c.1930. The bear's feet are flat, enabling him to stand. His neck is jointed but his body is unjointed; instead it has a metal armature running through it that allows the bear to be posed. **Ht 36cm (14in), £200–300 ($300–450)**

LES JOUETS ENCHANTÉS BEAR

Produced by the little-known French factory Les Jouets Enchantés in 1960, this rather simply made bear is fully jointed, hard stuffed and has large flat ears high on his head. During the 1950s and '60s there was a new range of unjointed bears made of synthetic fabric, which met with the new safety standards. **Ht 51cm (20in), £100–200 ($150–300)**

IDENTIFYING FEATURES

This clear glass eye is from the Fadap bear of 1930. Black button eyes were used by many French makers up until the 1930s.

This clear glass eye has an unusual white felt backing. It is from the unidentified bear of 1930 pictured far left on p.72.

OTHER MAKERS – IRISH & AUSTRALIAN

Irish bear making really began in 1938 when a government department established a subsidized industry manufacturing toys and small utility goods. There were three factories, one of which at Elly Bay, County Mayo, produced mohair teddy bears before World War II. The range of toys was called Erris Toys until 1953, when the name was changed to Tara Toys. Cheaper fabrics were used in the 1960s to compete with cheap imports but in 1979 Irish soft toy production ceased. In Australia teddy bears first became popular in the 1920s. Joy Toys and Fideston, both based in Melbourne, were two of the earliest manufacturers. Early bears were made of imported mohair, had glass eyes and were fully jointed, but the uniquely Australian unjointed stiff neck was quickly developed. World War II had a dramatic effect on toy production as the materials that were imported were almost impossible to obtain. New companies emerged after the war, such as Lindy Toys, but, sadly, by the 1970s, with the lifting of import tariffs, most Australian toy manufacturers went out of business.

TARA TOYS LAUGHING BEAR
Dating from 1953, this novelty bear is known as the laughing bear because his mouth opens and closes by moving a lever at the back of his head. Other notable features include the small, semi-circular ears that sit high on his head. The bear is made of gold mohair, his arms are curved, short and tapering and his chubby legs end in small feet with rexine pads. **Ht 41cm (16in), £250–350 ($375–525)**

TARA TOYS MUSICAL BEAR
This bear, c.1954, has a label (*see* above) saying "Made in the Republic of Ireland", which dates it to after 1949 because before that the word "Eire" was used. The distinctive nose stitching is typical of Tara Toys. **Ht 41cm (16in), £300–400 ($450–600)**

ERRIS TOYS BEAR

This bear is made of mohair and has a triangular-shaped head, glass eyes and a horizontally stitched nose. It also has a label saying "Made in Eire", which dates it to before 1949, when the company was still called Erris Toys (before changing to Tara Toys in 1953). Many of the Erris bears have embroidered labels with the manufacturer's name in Gaelic, which translated as Brèàgain Lorruis. **Ht 56cm (22in), £200–300 ($300–450)**

JOY TOYS BEAR

This very early Australian bear, c.1925, has a jointed neck. She also has pointed curved paws with cotton twill pads. Her clear glass eyes have painted backs and the nose stitching is similar to that of Chiltern, with long upward end stitches. Her petticoat is not original. Joy Toys was founded in the early 1920s in Victoria, Australia. The company was very successful and moved to a larger factory in 1930. **Ht 38cm (15in), £300–400 ($450–600)**

LATER SYNTHETIC BEAR

Also made by Joy Toys c.1970, this bear is made in bright gold synthetic plush and has a fixed stiff neck. His eyes are glass and his jointed arms and legs are short and plump and have rexine paw pads. His missing label originally would have been sewn into the seam on one of the paws. Labels were last used by the company in 1976. **Ht 30cm (12in), £100–150 ($150–225)**

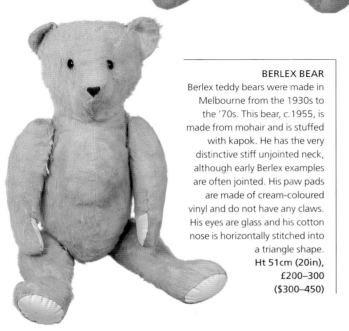

BERLEX BEAR

Berlex teddy bears were made in Melbourne from the 1930s to the '70s. This bear, c.1955, is made from mohair and is stuffed with kapok. He has the very distinctive stiff unjointed neck, although early Berlex examples are often jointed. His paw pads are made of cream-coloured vinyl and do not have any claws. His eyes are glass and his cotton nose is horizontally stitched into a triangle shape. **Ht 51cm (20in), £200–300 ($300–450)**

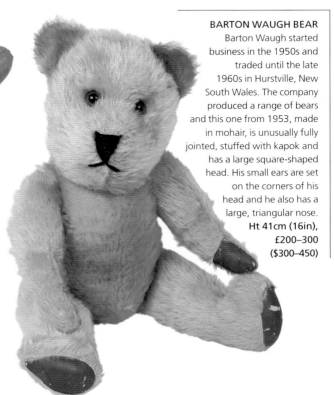

BARTON WAUGH BEAR

Barton Waugh started business in the 1950s and traded until the late 1960s in Hurstville, New South Wales. The company produced a range of bears and this one from 1953, made in mohair, is unusually fully jointed, stuffed with kapok and has a large square-shaped head. His small ears are set on the corners of his head and he also has a large, triangular nose. **Ht 41cm (16in), £200–300 ($300–450)**

ROOSEVELT BEARS

This page from a newspaper depicts Roosevelt bears. Prior to a book of 1906, stories of the Roosevelt bears were serialized in daily papers.

In 1902 US president Theodore Roosevelt went on a hunting expedition by the Mississippi river. After several days he had not shot a single bear and his hosts, in an effort to please him, searched the area until they found a bear cub, which they tied to a tree so that the president could go home with a trophy. However, Roosevelt refused to fire saying that he "drew the line" at killing a captured, defenceless bear as it was unsporting. When the story of this incident reached Clifford Berryman, a political cartoonist with *The Washington Post*, he drew a cartoon that appeared as part of a montage called "The Passing Show" on the front page of the newspaper. It depicted the president refusing to shoot the bear cub, with the caption "Drawing the line in Mississippi". The readers' response was overwhelming; they demanded more pictures of the bear and soon it appeared with Roosevelt in every picture Berryman drew.

TEDDY LORING, 1904 LAPEL PIN, ROOSEVELT PLATE AND PHOTOS
This rare Roosevelt plate was made from 1906 to 1908; they were given free with large mail orders from the Larkin Soap Co., USA, and very few now survive. The Teddy Loring bear, c.1910, is extremely desirable (*see* opposite); his pin is from the 1904 election campaign. The rare photographs are of Loring and Roosevelt. **Bear: ht 33cm (13in), £15,000+ ($22,500+). Plate: diam. 25cm (10in), £1,500–1,800 ($2,250–2,700)**

PILLOW COVER

This linen pillow cover, c.1905, shows two bears telephoning the White House. The dove of peace, a symbol used in Berryman's cartoons, holds the American flag and an olive branch. One bear is saying "Hello Central give me Teddy". At the turn of the century, when the telephone was still in its infancy, if people wished to make a call they went through "central", which was the main switchboard, and gave the number they wanted. The words were in the title of several popular songs at the time, such as *Hello Central, Give Me Heaven*". **Ht 51cm (20in), £450–550 ($675–825)**

BIRTH OF THE TEDDY BEAR

The early drawing had shown a large realistic bear tugging on a rope, but with each new cartoon the bear gradually changed until it had become a cute little cub, which Berryman called "the Roosevelt bear". Theodore Roosevelt, whose nickname was Teddy, became inextricably linked with the bear cub who became known as "Teddy's Bear", which was then shortened to "Teddy Bear". The teddy bear was adopted as a symbol for the presidential election campaign in 1904 and a whole array of campaign items, such as buttons and pins, were produced. Small mohair bears were mounted on stickpins and worn on lapels; these were distributed to the crowd when the president toured the country by train. Ceramic jugs and plates were decorated with political scenes involving bears: the president is often depicted in his uniform as lieutenant colonel of the first US volunteer cavalry, the "Rough Riders".

A bear called Teddy Loring is perhaps the closest link with Teddy Roosevelt. In 1909 the president went on a year-long trip to East Africa and among the party was a young naturalist, Alden Loring. On returning to the USA, the president gave a dinner in New York for those who had been on the trip and at the dinner a 33cm (13in) Steiff bear held the place card for each guest. Alden Loring took his home, and it remained in his family until the estate was sold in 1986.

IDEAL BEAR

This early bear, c.1904, has the same sideways-glancing googly eyes as the bear cub in the famous Berryman cartoons. This teddy is extremely rare and was probably given away to campaign supporters during the election. His collar and ribbon are original, but the remembrance badge was added when Roosevelt died in 1920. **Ht 25cm (10in), £3,000–4,000 ($4,500–6,000)**

TWO ROSA BEAR PLATES

These plates, c.1907, are part of the Rosa Bear series. They all have a political message and are linked to Teddy Roosevelt, who often appears on them as a very small figure dressed in the uniform of a rough rider. There is also a rhyme on each plate. The plate on the left, entitled "Up San Juan Hill", shows the bears as the rough riders, with the president leading them, and refers to the battle of San Juan Hill in the Spanish-American war of 1898. The plate on the right, called "The Bear Hunt", portrays the bears as the hunters. **Both: diam. 18cm (7in), £250–300 ($375–450) each**

COLOURED BEARS

This is a typical nose from a Chad Valley bear of 1930. It is triangular in shape, with vertical stitching and a horizontal top stitch.

Coloured bears are extremely popular with collectors now, but that was not always so. In the early years, before World War I, Steiff produced a few coloured bears but they were not a great success as customers preferred natural-coloured bears. Only a few early coloured Steiffs have survived, and they now command very high prices. In the years between the wars German makers such as Schuco, Jopi and Cramer made a wide range of coloured bears. British companies had received a huge boost to their business during and after World War I, due to the ban of German imports, and so began developing new ideas. Alternative fabrics were introduced, such as art silk (as used by Merrythought in seven different colours) and synthetic plush, and these were very popular, along with coloured mohair, right up until World War II. Chad Valley, in particular, are well-known for their coloured bears and some of their novelty bears, such as the Rainbow Tubby Bears series, were produced in dual colours.

RED CHAD VALLEY BEAR

This Chad Valley bear is made in mohair in a vivid shade of red. Unusually, the colour is unfaded; it is also interesting to note that his paw pads are made in red felt. He is the classic Chad Valley bear, having large flat ears, the typical Chad nose and a celluloid button in his ear. The red embroidered label on his foot dates him from 1930. Coloured bears in such good, all-original condition such as this are very rare. **Ht 46cm (18in), £1,800–2,200 ($2,700–3,300)**

BLUE CHAD VALLEY BEAR

Coloured bears reached the height of their popularity in the 1930s. Many of these bears were actually fashionable accessories for adults rather than toys. This blue bear, c.1930, has very thick mohair and he is in excellent condition. His mohair is slightly faded but in fact many of the blue bears that are found have hardly any colour left at all and it is only in the joints that can you see the true colour. So this bear has actually retained more colour than most. He also has a pristine foot label and a button in his ear. **Ht 46cm (18in), £1,500–2,000 ($2,250–3,000)**

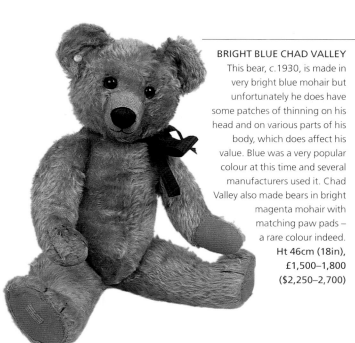

BRIGHT BLUE CHAD VALLEY
This bear, c.1930, is made in very bright blue mohair but unfortunately he does have some patches of thinning on his head and on various parts of his body, which does affect his value. Blue was a very popular colour at this time and several manufacturers used it. Chad Valley also made bears in bright magenta mohair with matching paw pads – a rare colour indeed.
Ht 46cm (18in), £1,500–1,800 ($2,250–2,700)

IDENTIFYING FEATURES

This celluloid button with blue lettering was used by Chad Valley in the 1930s. The idea of putting a button in the ear was originally Steiff's.

This red and white embroidered label was used by Chad Valley from the 1930s until 1938 when the Royal Warrant was issued (see p.22).

RAINBOW TUBBY BEAR
Made in the 1920s, this bear is a novelty bear from a Chad Valley series called the "Rainbow Tubby Bears". He has retained his original clown collar with the bells, but has lost his hat. These Tubby bears came in a variety of colours and sizes and had an hexagonal paper label attached to their chest with a ribbon and bell.
Ht 25cm (10in), £800–1,000 ($1,200–1,500)

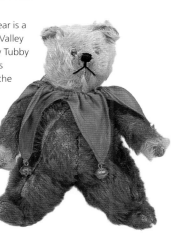

CLOWN BEARS
These two bears also belong to the "Rainbow Tubby Bears" clown series and date from 1925. The bear on the left has his original clown's hat and collar and his body and legs are rigid, allowing him to stand up unaided. The bear on the right is large for a Tubby bear; only his arms and head are jointed and his large body has been made all in one piece. He has lost his hat and collar. **Left:** ht 25cm (10in), £800–1,000 ($1,200–1,500). Right: ht 36cm (14in), £1,800–2,200 ($2,700–3,300)

WELL-LOVED RED BEAR
The many bald patches and the sparseness of his red mohair indicates that this Chad Valley bear, c.1930, has been very well loved. His nose has also been restitched, but he would still be desirable to a collector. When the plush is dyed with rich colours it weakens the material and wears out quickly – that is why so few coloured bears survive in perfect condition. **Ht 50cm (20in), £600–800 ($900–1,200)**

PINK SAMPLE BEAR
This very rare pink Chad Valley bear, made in 1931, was sent to Steiff as a sample of what Chad could produce. He differs from other Chads because he is very Steiff-like. He has long feet with nipped-in ankles and pink pads, and spoon-like paw pads. On returning from Steiff he was given to a Chad employee and remained in her family until recently. **Ht 66cm (26in), £2,000–2,500 ($3,300–3,750)**

COLOURED BEARS

TWO BLUE BEARS
These two blue bears are quite affordable – their condition is not pristine as the blue mohair is sparse in places but they are still very appealing. The bear on the left is an unjointed English bear from the 1950s by an unknown maker. He has quite a large head with cupped ears, glass eyes, vertical nose stitching with dropped-end stitches and unusual blue paw pads. On the right is a Chiltern bear from the 1930s. He has clear glass eyes and the typical Chiltern nose stitching (see p.25). **Ht: both 46cm (18in). Left: £200–300 ($300–450). Right: £300–400 ($450–600)**

RARE PINK CHILTERN BEAR
This lovely rose-pink Chiltern bear, c.1930, is quite rare as it is a difficult colour to find. He is in very good condition except for the fading on his head. The fact that the mohair on his body is unfaded indicates that he was probably dressed for many years. Most old bears are faded on the front of their bodies and head where they have been exposed to light. When you turn them over you can often see the original colour on the back. **Ht 50cm (20in), £700–800 ($1,050–1,200)**

BLUE MERRYTHOUGHT BEAR
Merrythought made a wide range of coloured bears and this blue mohair bear, c.1930, is a very good example. He has the distinctive Merrythought webbed claw stitching. During the 1930s Merrythought bears were also made of a new fabric called artificial silk. These bears often matched the clothes of the era and were carried around by fashion-conscious ladies. **Ht 50cm (20in), £700–900 ($1,050–1,350)**

RED, WHITE AND BLUE BEARS
Bears made in the patriotic colours of red, white and blue were very popular around the coronation of Queen Elizabeth II in 1953. The bear on the left, c.1955, has a centre seam down his face and a black oval shaped nose. The later bear on the right, c.1980, is by an unknown maker and is fully jointed. Both bears have kept their bright colours and would make an attractive addition to any collection. **Left:** ht 33cm (13in), £60–80 ($90–120). **Right:** 43cm (17in), £80–100 ($120–150)

TURQUOISE FARNELL BEAR
This Farnell bear, c.1920, has turquoise mohair that is much brighter on the back than on the front. He has the bulbous black glass eyes that are characteristic of Farnell and tan nose stitching. Farnell also used art silk for some coloured bears and registered their "Silkalite" trademark in 1929. **Ht 33cm (13in), £1,500–2,000 ($2,250–3,000)**

COLOURED ENGLISH BEAR
This is a very unusual coloured bear as he has both green and orange mohair. It is possible that when he was bought he had a clown's ruff around his neck. Clowns were very popular in the 1920s and 1930s and this bear by an unknown maker is c.1925. He is stuffed with mohair and wood wool, his feet have cardboard inserts and his paws are felt. He has a tilt growler that no longer works and his eyes are made of clear glass with painted backs. **Ht 46cm (18in), £1,500–2,000 ($2,250–3,000)**

DEAN'S CLOWN
This sweet clown bear, made by Dean's, has the "Childsplay" label, which dates him from after 1956, when production moved to Rye. He is unjointed except for the head and is made in cotton plush. He also has large, blue, plastic locked-in safety eyes. His clown's hat is stuffed and topped with a brass bell, his ears are set quite wide apart on his head and he has a very appealing expression. **Ht 36cm (14in), £200–400 ($300–600)**

BEARS WITH HISTORIES

This photo, taken in 1925, is of Evelyn May Yeoman and her daughter Zara, who is holding their treasured teddy bear, Bun.

When you find a bear with a known history it allows you a fascinating step back in time into a different era to share in the events that took place. The young owners of these bears were very devoted to them and were often photographed with them. As they grew into adulthood their bears remained faithful companions, as well as bringing joy to the next generation of children. In the early years of the 20th century many children died young from illness, and the horrors of World War I brought bereavement to many families. It is amazing how often the teddy bear was there to give comfort and consolation in times of grief. Many teddies survived through the bombs of World War II and some even went to war and suffered with their owners in prisoner-of-war camps. If you have a family teddy, or are acquiring one from an elderly owner, it is very important to write down his history because often it is handed down only by word of mouth. Likewise with family photos, as they get thrown away or the person's identity is forgotten. The ideal photograph is one of the owner with the bear, but if not then just the owner. Teddies with their histories are very desirable and more valuable, but alas they are few and far between.

BUN

Bun is a centre-seam cinnamon Steiff dating from 1908. He belonged to Evelyn May Yeoman, a great niece of the author Robert Louis Stevenson. As an adult Evelyn corresponded with Colonel Bob Henderson who owned Teddy Girl, the famous Steiff bear who fetched a record auction price of £110,000 in 1994. When Evelyn and Colonel Bob had tea together they were always accompanied by Bun and Teddy Girl. **Ht 40.5cm (16in), £5,000–6,000 ($7,500–9,000)**

DEVIZES TED

The photo shows Ted, a cinnamon Steiff bear, c.1910, with his owner Alfie William Harding, who was given Ted as a Christmas present when he was very young. Alfie married late in life and had no children and when he died in 1982 Ted was passed on to Alfie's brother, who kept him in a cellar. Eventually he was sold at auction in the market town of Devizes and fetched a provincial record sum. **Ht 63.5cm (25in), £8,000+ ($12,000+)**

BIG TED

This remarkable Steiff bear, c.1908, is in mint condition – even his tilt growler works. He belonged to the Cook children, seen in the photo, but he must have been a "Sunday" bear, played with only once a week. When the Cook family died out, Big Ted was left languishing in a trunk for many years until he was rescued. **Ht 63.5cm (25in), £12,000+ ($18,000+)**

NORAH'S BEAR

Norah's bear is a beautiful large Alpha Farnell from 1915. His owner, Norah Smith, who was born in 1911, is seen aged five pushing him in her doll's pram. She adored her bear and he was always given pride of place on her bed. When she grew up her own children were not allowed to play with him and therefore they had no affection for him. So when Norah died, sadly he was sold. **Ht 42cm (28in), £3,500–4,000 ($5,250–6,000)**

BABY ACHILLEA

This photo taken in 1911 shows two sisters, Daphne and Beryl Matchwick, aged eight and four years old standing in their garden in Reigate, Surrey. Beryl is holding her favourite bear, a mechanical Bing, c.1910, called Baby Achillea, named after the achillea flower. She was Beryl's constant companion throughout her life. **Ht 22.5cm (15in), £3,500–4,500 ($5,250–6,750)**

BEARS WITH HISTORIES

TEDDY ASHTON AND LITTLE TED

Teddy Ashton is a cinnamon Steiff dating from 1908. Here he is shown in a photo, taken in 1910, with his owner 10-year-old Elsie Ashton, who was one of four children. When two of her sisters tragically died, Elsie was given Teddy Ashton to console her. Little Ted, a bear by an unknown maker, c.1912, belonged to Elsie's brother, Cyril. When Cyril joined the army and went to France in World War I, Little Ted went with him, tucked into his jacket. Cyril survived the war but died in 1926 and Little Ted has lived with Teddy Ashton ever since. **Teddy Ashton: ht 40.5cm (16in), £5,000–6,000 ($7,500–9,000). Little Ted: 20cm (8in), £300–400 ($450–600).**

STEIFF POMERANIAN DOG

This Steiff Pomeranian dog-on-wheels is in mint condition, just as he was when he left the shop c.1907, but the reason for this is rather sad. He has a label reading "Christmas Greetings" and on the reverse is written "To Baby Francis from Aunt Adeline, with love". Unfortunately baby Francis died and the dog was packed away, carefully wrapped in tissue paper, and never played with. **Ht 28cm (11in), £2,000–2,500 ($3,000–3,750)**

PAM HEBBS' MUZZLE BEAR

This Steiff muzzle bear dates from 1913 and belonged to Pam Hebbs, a well-known and loved figure in the teddy bear world. Pam was one of the first dealers of vintage bears and her shop in Camden Passage, London, was a Mecca for teddy bear lovers from all over the world. Sadly, Pam died in 1999 and this muzzle bear now lives with a friend. **Ht 25.5cm (10in), £2,500+ ($3,750+)**

TEDDY BLACK

Teddy Black is a rare black Steiff from 1913. He is shown in the photo with his English owner, Hestor Drew. Teddy Black travelled to Gibraltar with Hestor when her father was posted there during World War I, and was a loving friend throughout her life. **Ht 51cm (20in), £15,000+ ($22,500+)**

PETER AND HIS FRIEND

Peter is an early Steiff bear, c.1908. He is pictured in the photo with the little girl who owned him and her younger brother. Peter was much loved and obviously played with as his paw pads had already been replaced when the picture was taken in 1918. His life-long friend is a bear, c.1910, by an unknown maker. **Peter: ht 35.5cm (14in), £1,500–2,000 ($2,250–3,000). Friend: ht 25.5cm (10in), £300–400 ($450–600)**

STEIFF BEAR-ON-WHEELS

This dear little bear-on-wheels dating from 1909 still has his original leather muzzle and his red felt saddle cloth. Only his head is jointed. He lived in an old cottage in West Sussex and the gentleman who owned him had no family so when he died the house was cleared and any photos that might have shown them together were thrown away. **Ht 25.5cm (10in), £1,500–2,000 ($2,250–3,000)**

BEAR NOVELTIES

WHAT TO LOOK FOR AND WHERE

• Bear novelties can be found at jumble or garage sales, boot fairs, doll and toy fairs, flea markets, teddy bear shows and country auctions.

• Early mechanical bear novelties can be expensive so keep an eye out for the newer pieces, made in the Far East.

• Teddy bear nightdress cases often turn up but can be quite expensive. Newer items such as handbags, rucksacks and even children's nursery chairs upholstered to look like bears can also be found.

Collecting bear novelties is a fascinating way to add diversity to your collection and there is plenty to choose from. Ever since the teddy bear was introduced, manufacturers have used their imagination to come up with new ideas for making novelty items. Many of them are by well-known makers such as Steiff, Bing and Schuco. Some teddy bear novelties were fashion accessories – such as purses, muffs and even mohair teddy bear coats made for children. There are bears that were made in the shape of glove puppets and others that are acrobatic, swinging on trapezes. Steiff was one of the companies that made a somersaulting bear and also, in 1907, they made a bear that had a hot-water bottle hidden in its body. These were unfortunately not very popular and so only 90 were ever made. Bears also appear as nightdress cases with zips up their backs and as handkerchief cases. These were both popular through the 1930s, '40s and '50s. Teddy bear novelties are still being made today and even teddy bear-shaped pasta is now available! It is great fun to go hunting for bear novelties and they will also add interest to your collection.

BABY BOTTLE HOLDER

This 1950s baby bottle holder bear was made by Else Sturm Co. of Ottobeuran, Germany. It is made of white mohair and still retains its original ribbon and label. The bear has amber and black glass eyes and a black stitched nose. His body unzips so that the baby's bottle can be put inside. Some bottle holders also came with a voice box in the bottom of the holder; this one has a squeaker that was activated when a baby drank from the bottle. **Ht 28cm (11in), £75–85 ($110–125)**

ROLY POLY CLOWN BEAR

This charming 1930 Roly Poly clown bear is by an unknown maker but is probably German. During the 1930s clowns were very popular and bears often appeared with clowns' hats and ruffs on. This one has a red and green felt body over a celluloid inner shell, which contains a chime mechanism that plays when he is rolled. His collar has bells on it and he also has a satin ruff. **Ht 18cm (7in), £350–450 ($525–675)**

STEIFF ROLY POLY

Steiff Roly Poly bears are very sought after by collectors and this 1908 one is a delightful example. He is made of mohair and has the typical early Steiff head. He sits on a round weighted base, so that when he is pushed over he springs back again and the rattle inside his body shakes. Steiff made other Roly Poly toys in the form of clowns, rabbits, cats and even gollies. **Ht 18cm (7in), £4,000–6,000 ($6,000–9,000)**

SLEEPY-EYED BEAR

This American bear has celluloid googly eyes that close when he tilts his head back. His manufacturer is not known but similar bears with movable eyes were made by an American maker called The National French and Novelty Co. This 1920 bear is made in gold mohair and has a shaved muzzle with black nose stitching. He has a plump body with short arms and felt paw pads, and is hard stuffed with wood wool. **Ht 41cm (16in), £1,200–1,500 ($1,800–2,250)**

STEIFF SOMERSAULTING BEAR

This is a rare, white mohair, somersaulting bear from 1909. Such bears were usually gold or dark brown. This bear has a clockwork mechanism that is activated by winding the left arm, causing him to go head over heels. He has hooks on his paws that can be attached to a trapeze, which he will then tumble over continuously. **Ht 25cm (10in), £2,000–2,500 ($3,000–3,750)**

TEDDY BEAR PURSE

This delightful teddy bear purse from 1912 was intended for use by a child. There is a metal frame and a chain to hold the purse by and the inside is lined with cotton. The bear has a jointed head, arms and legs and is made of short gold mohair. He also has brown and black glass eyes and horizontal nose stitching. Bear purses such as this one were made in Germany and the USA. **Ht 20cm (8in), £1,000–1,200 ($1,500–1,800)**

WIND-UP BEAR

This very early wind-up bear from 1910 is by an unknown German maker and depicts a performing bear. This was a very popular subject for bear makers during this period, as performing bears were a common sight all around Europe. He is made of papier mâché covered in silk plush. His muzzle has a chain attached to it and when he is wound up he plays the accordion. **Ht 20cm (8in), £400–500 ($600–750)**

BEAR NOVELTIES

STEIFF'S FLUFFY THE CAT
Produced c. 1926, Fluffy the Cat is made in tipped mohair, which gives her a very natural appearance. Her face and chest are white mohair, the nose stitching is pink and her eyes are green glass with black pupils. The pillow Fluffy is attached to is made of faded blue mohair and the whole item is very rare, hence the price. **Ht 15cm (6in), £2,000–2,500 ($3,000–3,750)**

CHEEKY MUFF
This unusual Merrythought Cheeky muff, c. 1967, is very appealing. His head and legs are made of gold mohair and he has a velvet muzzle. The muff itself is white plush. He has a wide, smiling Cheeky mouth that is stitched in black silk, and wide-apart ears that have bells in them. Cheeky bears were made in various other colours and also appeared as nightdress cases. **Ht 25cm (10in), £250–350 ($375–525)**

TEDDY BEAR PILLOW
This novelty pillow, c. 1920, was made by an unknown maker but most were produced in the USA. It is doubtful whether the pillow was ever used, as it seems simply to be a decorative item. It is made of short bristle mohair and the bear's head is stuffed with wood wool. His ears are small and he has black nose stitching. **Size 20 x 20cm (8 x 8in), £300–400 ($400–600)**

PINK MUFF
The vibrant pink mohair of this child's muff is in excellent condition for its age, as it dates from 1939. The muff is lined with cotton and has a purse hidden in the back, as well as a press squeaker in each foot. The bear's eyes are black and white, which is unusual because most were amber and black at the time. Children's muffs were particularly popular during the 1920s and '30s. **Ht 25cm (10in), £200–300 ($300–450)**

BEAR WITH SHOES
This unusual-looking bear is by an unknown maker but dates from 1930. He has felt shoes sewn onto his mohair legs, which are very large in proportion to his body. His ears are also very big and are lined with a contrasting colour mohair. He must have been dressed at one time because his torso is made of cotton. **Ht 36cm (14in), £100–200 ($150–300)**

TEDDY MUFF
This is an early, c.1912, teddy bear muff made in gold mohair. It was fashionable at the time for children to wear teddy bear coats and hats that were made of gold or even white mohair. A muff like this one completed the outfit. **Ht 30cm (12in), £400–500 ($600–750)**

BEAR HANDKERCHIEF CASE
This bear was made in England, c.1950, at a time when mohair was in short supply. Makers saved on mohair by incorporating other fabrics. Here only the head, paws and feet are mohair – the dress is made of pink wool and cotton. This item was made for storing handkerchiefs. **Ht 36cm (14in), £200–300 ($300–450)**

WINNIE-THE-POOH PURSE
This contemporary evening purse is by the famous designer Katherine Bauman of Los Angeles. It is made entirely of Swarovski Austrian crystal and is part of a limited edition of 2,500. **Ht 14cm (5½in), £2,500–3,000 ($3,750–4,500)**

MUSICAL BEARS

The paw pads on Moritz Pappe bears have four black silk claws stitched very closely together on the mohair.

Musical bears were made by many manufacturers, both in Europe and the USA, and these charming bears are eagerly sought after by many collectors. Some of the German makers in particular specialized in musical bears during the 1920s and '30s and made many in vibrant colours and tipped mohair. Some of these bears contained a squeeze-box musical movement in their tummy that was activated by pressing it, but by the 1930s key-wind clockwork music boxes were introduced instead. Josef Pitrmann of Jopi is famous for his musical bears made during this period. However, of the huge number of musical bears that were made, few are easily identified. At one time it was thought that some were made by Helvetic, but that is only the name that is stamped on the music box itself. Helvetic is actually now used to describe a type of musical bear from the 1920s and '30s. Musical bears were popular in Britain in the 1950s and '60s; the English company Chiltern introduced their famous Ting-a-ling Bruin in the 1950s, which had a mechanism that produced a tinkling sound when shaken.

MORITZ PAPPE BEAR
Moritz Pappe was a German manufacturer of dolls who, from 1910, produced bears as well. A somersaulting bear that was similar to Steiff's (*see* p.87) was made in 1911. Pappe also made clown bears, coloured art silk bears and bears with musical movements in the 1920s and '30s. This bear, *c.*1928, has a squeeze-box movement. Many such bears have been wrongly identified as Helvetic. **Ht 33cm (13in), £900–1,000 ($1,350–1,500)**

PAIR OF GERMAN CATS
The sitting cat on the left is in tipped mohair and has a squeeze-box movement. He is possibly by Jopi. Puss-in-Boots on the right is by an unknown German maker. He too has a squeeze-box movement. Both are *c.*1927. **Left: ht 20cm (8in), £700–800 ($1,050–1,200). Right: ht 51cm (20in), £1,000–1,200 ($1,500–1,800)**

PAIR OF UNKNOWN BEARS

These attractive, coloured musical bears, *c*.1930, would be highly favoured by collectors. Both have squeeze-box mechanisms and the one on the left has a clown's ruff. Musical bears are often found dressed as clowns and these are probably German examples. **Left:** ht 30cm (12in), £800–900 ($1,200–1,350). **Right:** ht 38cm (15in), £1,000–1,200 ($1,500–1,800)

EDUARD CRÄMER BEAR

The musical movement of this *c*.1930 bear is activated by moving the head up and down. He is hard stuffed with wood wool and is made in golden mohair. Such bears are very rare. Eduard Cramer was a German maker who designed some very distinctive bears, such as those with heart-shaped inserts on their faces or ones with embroidered felt tongues. **Ht** 30cm (12in), £2,000–2,500 ($3,000–3,750)

BLUE-TIPPED BEAR

This German bear has wonderful deep, blue-tipped mohair. It is a very desirable bear as it is rare to find mohair in such an unfaded condition. He was probably made by Jopi, *c*.1925, and has a squeeze-box movement. His long narrow feet have velvet paw pads, which is typical of this type of bear. **Ht** 25cm (10in), £1,200–1,500 ($1,800–2,250)

ALPHA FARNELL CAT

Dating from 1935, this seated cat has a wind-up musical movement and a blue and white Alpha Farnell label. Only his head is jointed and he is stuffed with wood wool; he has gold glass eyes and an embroidered nose. Cats by famous makers are highly collectable items. **Ht** 25cm (10in), £200–300 ($300–450)

TWO MUSICAL BEARS

These two musical bears, *c*.1925, have distinctive shaved muzzles, small ears on the side of their wide heads, batwing-shaped nose stitching and no mouths. They are examples of the bear type often called Helvetic. This is probably because of the stamp on the squeeze-box musical movement but, in fact, they are by an unknown German maker. **Ht** 30cm (12in), £1,800–2,000 ($2,700–3,000) each

NEW BEARS

JEFFERSON BY FRANK WEBSTER
Jefferson is one of a series of Charnwood Bears made by this very well-known bear artist. He is a one-of-a-kind bear made in the traditional style, with very big feet and a shaved muzzle. Frank Webster's bears are much in demand and limited editions such as this one will be highly sought after. **Ht 54cm (21in), £195 ($295) new**

MANUFACTURED BEARS

Manufactured bears fall into various categories. There are old makers, such as Steiff and Merrythought, who produce limited-edition replicas of their original designs, as well as new creations. Some also employ well-known teddy bear artists to design limited-edition bears for them, enabling collectors to acquire a bear by a famous artist at a very reasonable price. Many new makers, such as Russ, have sprung up in the USA and Europe to meet the huge demand for teddy bears, some of which operate in the Far East. These bears are usually very affordable and within the reach of most collectors, and the quality and design is excellent. Many manufacturers produce two ranges – one that is washable and child-safe and a collectors' range, offering something for everyone. The prices given are average retail values.

REPLICA OF 1962 BEAR BY CLEMENS

Clemens' first bears were made from blankets left over from World War II; today their bears are handmade from the finest materials to the highest standards and the West German company is now enjoying more popularity than ever. The bear pictured left is a replica of design that was originally produced in 1962. He is 42cm (16½in), made in high-quality pointed mohair and is fully jointed, with a squeaker inside. His stuffing is soft, making him very cuddly. **£100 ($150) new**

FIPS BY CLEMENS

Fips is a millennium bear designed by Martina Lehr, one of a number of artists working for Clemens. He is 25cm (10in) high and was made in a limited edition of 2,000. He is made of top-quality honey-coloured mohair and has a large nose with downward stitching. He is fully jointed and is sitting in an unusual pose on a money sack, gazing optimistically into the future. The hessian sack he sits on is filled with pellets and 20 German pfennig coins. **£100 ($150) new**

BARLEY FROM DEAN'S ELITE RANGE

Dean's Elite range is one of their newest, and was set up in order to make use of the huge variety of more unusual mohairs available today. They only make a very limited edition of each bear – there are just 75 Barleys in existence. Each Elite bear has a special sewn label and comes with a certificate. Barley is 61cm (24in) high and is the largest bear in the range. He is made from curly tipped beige mohair and is partially bean-filled, giving him a nice rounded look. **£345 ($520) new**

TIGER TOES BY JILL BAXTER FOR DEAN'S

This limited-edition bear was designed by the famous English artist Jill Baxter for Dean's Artist Showcase range. In 1991 Dean's managing director, Neil Miller, invited bear artists to submit photographs of their work for possible inclusion in the range. Now in its sixth year, the range is highly prestigious and successful. Jill has a distinctive style and the bear shown here is a typical example. It is made from an unusual copper-tipped curly mohair and is 53cm (21in) high. **£250 ($375) new**

WILLS BY GUND

Gund is America's oldest soft toy company, and has been around for almost 100 years. This bear is from their new Mohair Collection and was produced as a limited edition of 400. He is 30cm (12in) high, soft stuffed and is made of light beige mohair with a khaki backing. Wills' arms are longer than his legs and he has velveteen paws and soles. He also has an embroidered nose, beans in his bottom and feet and is wearing a traditional chequered ribbon. **£135 ($200) new**

CREME DE LA BEAR BY GUND

This 30cm (12in) bear is based on Gund's one-of-a-kind Centennial Bear that was auctioned for charity in the autumn of 1998. He is made from the same exclusive mohair as the original and his paw pads are velveteen topped with suede cloth. Fully jointed, he has a gentle expression and a luxurious feel. The bear comes packaged in a box that has the same award-winning graphics on it as can be found on Gund packaging from the 1930s, '40s and '50s. **£25 ($40) new**

LIMITED-EDITION TEDDY BEAR BY HERMANN

Gebrüder Hermann was established in 1907 in Hirschaid, Germany. Every Hermann bear carries the trademark red badge with Hermann Teddy Original written on it. Thousands of teddies leave the factory today for destinations worldwide, made by skilled workers using only the finest-quality handmade fabrics. This bear is one of a limited edition of 2001 pieces. He is 45cm (18in) high, fully jointed and made of unopened caramel mohair, with a growler inside. **£105 ($160) new**

YESTERDAY BY HERMANN

This bear is another new design from the old German company, Gebrüder Hermann. He is 51cm (20in) high and was made as a limited edition of 2,000. The bear is made of unusual string mohair, which has been manufactured on authentic old machines from the 1920s. His black nose is handstitched and his paws and pads are made of felt. He is jointed, has a growler and is stuffed with wood wool. His small companion is a replica of a 1950s kitten. **£130 ($195) new**

REPLICA OF FREDDIE FARNELL BY MERRYTHOUGHT

This is a replica of a 1930s Alpha Farnell that is actually owned by the author, Sue Pearson (*see* p.129). The replica was made as a limited edition of 250. He was copied exactly from the original bear and even his size, 66cm (26in), is the same. Merrythought acquired the right to use the name of Alpha Farnell on replica bears in 1996, and under the left arm of each limited edition there is a tag giving the number of the bear as well as a guarantee of quality. **£295 ($440) new**

21ST-CENTURY BEAR BY MERRYTHOUGHT

This bear was designed by Jacqueline Revitt for Merrythought to commemorate the start of the new century. He is embellished with an engraved Merrythought 21st-century solid silver button, which bears the Birmingham Assay Office hallmark and the official hallmark of Merrythought Limited. He is 46cm (18in) high, fully jointed and made of beautiful golden-feathered mohair, with amber eyes and hand-embroidered features. Only 1,000 were made. **£190 ($285) new**

RUGGLES BY NORTH AMERICAN BEAR COMPANY, INC.

Barbara Isenberg and her brother Paul Levy founded this toy company in New York in 1978 and it has now become a hugely successful, international name. As well as teddy bears, NABCO produce a wide range of other plush toys and accessories. These two unjointed bears are called Ruggles – one is 63.5cm (25in) high and the smaller of the two measures 43cm (17in) in height – and they are part of the Classic range of plush bears. **Left: £22 ($35) new. Right: £55 ($85) new**

MUFFY VANDERBEAR BY NORTH AMERICAN BEAR COMPANY, INC.

Muffy is probably the most famous of NABCO's bears. She joined the existing VanderBear family in 1984 and became a celebrity so quickly that an international fan club was set up in her honour. As well as the Muffy bear, there are many different Muffy outfits to collect and a wide range of Muffy accessories, from calendars to t-shirts. Muffy herself measures 18cm (7in) in height and is fully jointed, with golden yellow mohair and her signature blue ribbon. **£14 ($20) new**

TENNYSON BY RUSS BERRIE AND CO. INC.

Founded in the early 1970s, with distribution centres across the USA, in Canada and in the UK, Russ Berrie is the largest toy gift company in the world, producing "impulse" gifts that customers cannot resist. Tennyson is from their "Bears from the Past" collection. He is unjointed and is made in cream plush. He is a floppy bean bear and is suitable for both children and adult collectors. He is 46cm (18in) high and has a navy and white chequered bow around his neck. **£15 ($22) new**

BARTHOLOMEW BY RUSS BERRIE AND CO. INC.

This 30cm (12in) bear is part of Russ' Vintage Mohair Collection. He is golden wheat-coloured, made of mohair and is fully jointed. He is filled with beans and has hand-embroidered features, tan suedeen paw pads and a peach muslin bow. He has a worn nose and "repair stitches" over his body that have been used to make him look old. He is a limited edition of 25,000 and comes with a vintage-edition button on his wrist and a certificate of authenticity. £37 ($55) new

REPLICA OF 1928 PETSY BEAR BY STEIFF

Probably the most famous of all teddy bear manufacturers, Steiff is still a thriving company today. They make a wide range of bears and animals, all of which use high-quality materials of European origin. This bear is one of a collection of replica bears that Steiff produce. Part of a limited edition of 4,000, he is 36cm (14in) high and made of tipped mohair. His chest tag, a copy of the original, says "Petsy 1928 Replica". As with all Steiffs, he has a brass button in his ear. £160 ($240) new

HARRODS CENTENARY BEAR BY STEIFF

Steiff produce an annual bear that is sold exclusively by Harrods, London. Traditional in design, this bear of 1995 is a limited edition of 2,000 pieces and has a wind-up musical mechanism that plays the *Anniversary Waltz* to commemorate 100 years of the partnership between Steiff and Harrods. Fully jointed and 43cm (17in) tall, he is made of green mohair with felt pads and a paisley silk cravat pinned with a gold Steiff pin. He has the Steiff button and white tag in his ear. £185 ($280) new

ARTIST BEARS

Collecting artist bears is a very popular pastime and there is a vast range of designs to choose from, providing something for everyone. The idea of bear artists began in the USA in the 1970s as a spin off from doll making and it quickly spread to the UK during the 1980s. Now there are artists all over the world creating the most imaginative and wonderful bears. A bear artist is an individual who designs and makes bears, sometimes with help but very often single-handedly. This means an artist bear is not the same as a manufactured bear that was made in a factory in large quantities. Each artist bear carries a label stating the name of the maker and the bear, and whether it is a limited edition or even a one-off piece. Occasionally an open-edition bear is made that is available for some time. However, artists are not able to produce bears in very large numbers so some patience is necessary if ordering a special bear – there is sometimes a wait of up to a year for one made by a well-known artist. It is possible to buy an artist bear for just a few pounds or dollars, or to pay several hundred for a bear if it is made by one of the more famous makers. Many of these talented artists attend the teddy bear shows that are held all over the world, providing a hunting ground for beginners and collectors alike.

SALLY LAMBERT

Sally began by making dolls' house miniatures and then moved on to miniature bears. Her first bears were sold in 1995 at a dolls' house miniatures fair and she has had a full order book ever since. The bears range in size from 1.25cm (½in) to 7.6cm (3in) and Sally exhibits one-off pieces and limited editions at teddy bear shows in the UK, Japan and the USA. In 1999 she won the miniaturist category at the British Bear Artist Awards and was awarded for the most original entry. Collectors can view Sally's bears in museums worldwide and buy them at shows or by mail order. Sally also designs for major manufacturers.

TWO BEARS RIDING ON A SWAN (winner of a 2001 US Toby award)
They are made from plush fabrics combined with ultra-suede and filled with polyester stuffing; the swan is 10cm (4in) high. Sally has used onyx beads for the eyes and the flowers on their heads are made of silk. **£400 ($600) new**

PORTOBELLO BEARS

Amy Goodrich was inspired by the materials and artefacts found in the markets of London and Paris during her studies at art college. This led her on to designing bears, each with an individual character and personality. Amy specializes in hand cross-stitched sampler bears, made from vintage chenille, appliqué and embroidery – creating unique bears out of fabulous textiles. Long-haired "realistic" bears and various animals are also in her repertoire. Amy's award-winning Portobello Bears can be found at fairs in London and San Diego, California, through various stockists or direct from Amy herself.

DARLING PEGGY
Peggy has wooden joints, wood wool and polyfibre stuffing, aged suedette pads and hand-blown glass eyes. She is 60cm (24in) high and is covered in English mohair and her clothes are made from vintage fabrics. **£495 ($740) new**

SHOEBUTTON BEARS

Ten years ago Sue Wilkes visited a teddy bear fair with her daughter where she bought some joints, eyes and mohair and began designing bears. At that time she was teaching crafts at night school and decided that mohair was too expensive but that pipe-cleaners would make the perfect material for her students to use. Sue then began to dress her pipe-cleaner bears and now makes a wide range of bears, gollies, cats, dogs and rabbits. She has a regular stall at the annual Hugglets Fairs in London (*see* pp.152–153) and also supplies a number of shops in the UK and abroad.

SCHOOLBOY AND SCHOOLGIRL
These two schoolchildren are very well turned out in their uniforms and real leather satchels. Each bear is only 6cm (2in) high but the attention to detail on the bears and their clothing is meticulous. **£15 ($22) each new**

STRAWBEARIES

Kathy Harry began her bear-making career almost eight years ago and it has now become a full-time labour of love for both herself and her husband Rob, who helps out with many aspects of the business. They work all year round to keep up with the high demand that Kathy's bears now attract. The bears range in size from 5cm (2in) to 100cm (40in) and most of them are made from dyed mohair. Kathy's bears can be ordered and are also sold at shows and selected shops in Australia, the UK and Singapore. Look for the "StrawBearies" pin attached to each bear for a guarantee of originality and authenticity.

GWENDOLINE
With her love of millinery and a fascination in the fashions of the 1920s, it is inevitable that many of Kathy's bears have cloche hats adorned with vintage flowers, netting and ribbons, as on this 24-cm (9½-in) bear. **£120 ($180) new**

JOAN WOESSNER

Joan started making bears in 1983 while part owner of a craft store in California, USA. She then began to teach bear making, using her own patterns and supplying the necessary materials for her students, some of whom have become popular artists themselves today. In 1986 Joan took her bears to a show in San Diego and, as a result of receiving many orders, set up a wholesale business to cope with the demand. Joan has received numerous awards including Artist of the Year from the International League of Teddy Bear Clubs and two Toby Awards at Walt Disney World's Doll & Teddy Bear Convention.

VICTORIAN LADY
This elegant bear, 16.5cm (6½in) high, is dressed in pure silk trimmed with lace. The artist has given her an elaborate hat decorated with flowers and she carries a parasol, as befits a lady of the Victorian period. **£135 ($200) new**

JO GREENO

Jo Greeno began her career as a teacher but she started to make bears professionally in 1990. Based in Surrey, England, Jo is invited to give presentations, judge competitions, teach and exhibit as far afield as Japan, Singapore, the USA and Australia. Her work has featured in publications and videos and it is her one-off designs, characterized by cartoon-like faces with large close-set eyes and smiling mouths, that are much sought after by collectors. She also occasionally designs bears for Dean's Rag Book Co. Since 1993 Jo has been a member of the editorial team for *Teddy Bear Times* magazine.

COVER GIRL

Both Cover Girl and the purse around her neck are made of mohair. She is 61cm (24in) tall, with flexi-limb arms that can be posed and the instantly recognisable Jo Greeno features of large close-set eyes and a smiley mouth. **£750 ($1,125) new**

FLUFF AND STUFF

Kay Turmeau has been making soft toys since the age of ten but it wasn't until 1991 that she plucked up enough courage to launch her own business making teddy bears. She was awarded an Enterprise Allowance and officially launched "Fluff and Stuff" in 1992. Most of the bears she now makes are between 13cm (5in) and 25cm (10in). Kay works alone in Berkshire, England, with her dog and the radio for company – it is the latter that often provides her with inspiration as an interesting programme will spark off a design idea. Her bears are collected all over the world, particularly in the Far East and USA.

GRACIE AND TIMMY TOMPKINS

Gracie, on the left, is 15cm (6in) high and one-of-a-kind and Timmy Tompkins is a 13-cm (5-in) limited-edition bear of 20 pieces. Both mohair bears are fully jointed, with boot-button eyes. **Left: 130 ($195) new. Right: £120 ($180) new**

CHRISTINE PIKE BEARS

Christine's interest in bears was fuelled by a school holiday project on the history of toys. Since then she has been a keen collector of antique and artist bears and dolls and also studied the restoration of such items as a teenager. She became a bear artist in 1995 and now sells and exhibits her work worldwide. When she is designing a new bear at her home on the Isle of Wight, Christine prefers to make sketches from photographs of real bears. The resulting soft bears always reflect realistic proportions, which means they have small heads, large bodies and huge feet; collectors are always amazed at how lifelike they look.

DIM-SUM

Dim-Sum is a 41-cm (16-in) panda made in gold and brown/black-tipped mohair. He has a double-jointed neck, a leather nose, sculpted teeth and eyelids and plush, needle-sculpted paw pads to emphasise his toes. **£375 ($565) new**

BALLYTHREAD BEAR

Ballythread bears are made by Leila Stewart in County Mayo, Ireland. She began making bears by following patterns from craft magazines and books, but when she attended the 1990 Kensington Bear Show she was overawed by the quality of the bears there and decided to concentrate on making clothes for bears. She made a few fur bears in order to size her clothes, and most of these were given as presents to friends. She had purchased a small amount of mohair from the 1990 show and when she finally used it realized she had a talent for bear making. Since then she has made traditional, one-off bears.

H.J.
This bear was commissioned as a one-off for a friend of the artist, called H.J., and he is in the style of an antique German bear. Made in mohair, he is 43cm (17in), fully jointed and dressed in a tweed waistcoat and bow tie. **£150 ($225) new**

ORIGINAL RICA-BÄR

Ulrike Charles is a part-time teacher in Germany. Her hobbies have included painting, knitting, designing and dressmaking but it wasn't until relatively recently that she turned her hand to making teddy bears. Her first bears were given as presents to friends and relatives but she then decided to offer a wider choice to the public and created the Original Rica-Bär. Her bears are all originals but have a classic feel as they are made from mohair and have either antique shoe-button eyes or Austrian glass eyes. They are small, limited editions or one-of-a-kind pieces and are usually dressed in vintage-style clothes.

ALEXANDER
This jaunty bear, 44cm (17in) high, is made from dense German mohair filled with polyfill and pellets. His eyes are antique shoe buttons and he wears antique linen dungarees and cap, and a pair of children's boots. **£160 ($240) new**

MINIKINS

Maggie Spackman runs Minikins, her own miniature bear company in Hertfordshire, England. All her bears are handmade and over the years she has experimented with fabrics and patterns to develop her own unique style. Maggie says that she concentrates on getting as much movement, character and originality into each bear as possible and they often have strong themes to them. She mainly uses American fabrics to dress the bears, as she likes the colours and prints that are available. She sells her work around the world and also has several bears on display at the Puppenhausmuseum in Basel, Switzerland.

YOSEMITE
This bear is made from American long-pile upholstery velvet, with ultra-suede pads and muzzle, onyx-bead eyes and an embroidered silk nose. He is 10cm (4in) high and wears a handwoven coat with knitted sleeves. **£185 ($280) new**

NORBEARY BEARS

Gloria Norbury, from Lancashire, England, had long been a serious collector of all types of Victorian toys and dolls before she turned her attention to bears in 1988. She had developed a sense of wanting to recreate "old world" charm when she spent time restoring her Victorian purchases and used this same approach with her teddy bears. She developed her own style, creating forlorn ragamuffins. These bears are at times outrageously distressed and are often dressed in shabby items of clothing. However, such bears truly express her love of old playthings. Gloria's bears have inspired countless other bear makers.

JESSICA AND DAPHNE

These love-lorn, floppy bears convey a magical old-time appeal, with their vintage hats and loose-textured mohair. Jessica is 43cm (17in) high and Daphne is slightly smaller at 38cm (15in). **Left: £120 ($180) new. Right: £95 ($145) new**

SOMETHINGS BRUIN

Jill Baxter started making bears in 1993. Having come from an artistic background, the designs came easily but the production of the faces took several attempts until she was satisfied. The moulds are made from a sculpture, then a copy is made, covered with felt and airbrushed. Jill began by making traditional-looking bears, but her style has evolved into a much more modern look. Most of the bears' faces incorporate a huge Roman nose and close-set eyes. The feet are large, as are the tummies, and the ears hang from the side of the head to give each bear a comical expression. Jill designs for Dean's Artist Showcase (see p.95).

LION

This mohair lion is one of a limited-edition of four pieces. He has a moulded felt-covered face with air brushed details and sewn fingers and toes. He is 40.5cm (16in) high and stuffed with polyester and polyester beads. **£195 ($295) new**

FAIRY CHUCKLE – HIRO TAKAHASHI

Fairy Chuckle is run by Hiro and Michi Takahashi of Japan. They were both enchanted by bears while on their honeymoon and decided to start making their own. Hiro made his first bear to celebrate their third wedding anniversary. Since then, his bears have been displayed all around the world, particularly in the UK. He was in fact the first male Japanese teddy bear artist. When he started out, teddy bear making was not popular in Japan so he had to import mohair all the way from the USA and the UK. He makes each of his bears by hand, they are always undressed and every bear is a unique, one-of-a-kind.

MOTHER AND COY CUBS IN HUDSON BAY

These polar bears were inspired by a trip to Hudson Bay, Canada. They are 20cm (8in) high, made of white German mohair with poly-fibre stuffing. The cubs cling to their mother, expressing their intimate relationship. **£1,300 ($1,950) new**

FAIRY CHUCKLE – MICHI TAKAHASHI

Michi Takahashi started exhibiting her teddy bears in 1993 in Britain, the USA, Japan, Australia and the Netherlands. Examples of her work have appeared in numerous books and she has been nominated for various awards. In 1996 her Over the Rainbow bear was sold for approximately £4,650 ($7,000) in the Berryman's International Teddy Bear Artists' Auction, which was a record-breaking amount for a Japanese artist. Each of Michi's bears is lovingly made by hand from patterns that she creates herself and are often made in small, limited editions. They are also usually dressed in beautiful Japanese costumes.

SAKURA
This exquisite bear is dressed in a traditional Japanese silk kimono. One-of-a-kind, she is 48cm (19in) high, fully jointed, made of mohair and has ultra-suede paw pads. She is wearing traditional handmade wooden clogs. **£2,400 ($3,600) new**

COMPANION BEARS

Since starting to make bears in 1994, Elaine Lonsdale has established herself as one of Britain's leading bear artists, based in Cheshire, England. She won Best New Artist at the British Bear Artist Awards in 1995 and since then has collected many other awards from both England and the USA. Elaine used to be a retail window dresser and also had her own vintage clothes shop. This background fuelled her talent for creating unusual, entirely unique designs. Even if she uses a design or material for the second time, she always ensures that each bear is very different from anything else that she has made previously.

TWO HATTED BEARS
These two mohair bears are dressed in fabrics that have been hand-tinted by the artist. Their hats are made of Irish linen, trimmed with antique fabric flowers, and their eyes are onyx beads. They both measure 15cm (6in). **£350 ($525) each**

CHANGLE BEARS, SOUTH AFRICA

Janet Changfoot was encouraged into bear making by a friend. Having an artistic background, she took to it quickly and began experimenting with an airbrush. She found that she could use this to enhance her bears' faces. Each bear is either one-of-a-kind or part of a very limited edition and they have won her awards in South Africa and England. She views the highlight of her career so far as winning a British Bear Artist Award in 2000. Her bears are made of mohair, have glass eyes and are fully jointed. They range in height from 13cm (5in) to 61cm (24in).

SHIRAZ
In order to achieve Shiraz's lovely golden colour, the artist hand-dyed the German mohair used to make this cuddly bear. He is 30.5cm (12in) tall, with an embroidered nose, black glass eyes and airbrushed features. **£135 ($200) new**

OTHER BEARS
&
THEIR FRIENDS

LARGE STEIFF MICKEY MOUSE
Steiff made a number of Mickey Mouse toys between 1931 and 1936. This large-sized version, c.1932, has the typical "cherry-pie" eyes and is extremely sought after. **Ht 43cm (17in)**, £1,500–2,000 ($2,250–3,000)

GOLLIES

HOW TO RECOGNIZE AND DATE A GOLLY

• Very early gollies have protruding noses that were stitched on, eyes mostly made from linen buttons and smiling red mouths.

• The hair on early gollies is often rabbit fur or sealskin. They were also usually homemade, except for the Steiff golly.

• Later gollies are flat faced, often with button eyes, their hair is made of plush or wool and they are mostly unjointed. Often they are dressed in jackets, waistcoats, striped trousers and bow ties.

• Gollies from the 1950s and '60s have plastic eyes and synthetic fabric.

The golly made his first appearance in a book called *The Adventures of the Two Dutch Dolls* by Florence Upton, which was published in 1895. Florence was born in the USA in 1873 to English parents who had emigrated there from Hampstead, London. It was on a visit to England that Florence was given a black rag doll by her grandmother. This doll inspired her in later years, after the family had returned to England, to create a black character called the "golliwogg" as a friend for her wooden Dutch dolls. Florence was a talented artist and painted 31 pictures of the golliwogg and her wooden dolls. Her mother, Bertha, wrote a series of verses to go with the pictures and the finished work was published in 1895. It was an immediate success as the golliwogg captured children's imagination. The duo went on to write 12 more books over the next 14 years. However, Florence did not copyright her golliwogg and soon various golly dolls appeared. Other authors began to write books featuring gollies alongside children, animals and teddy bears. Golly dolls have continued to be made up to the present day and some companies have begun making replicas of their old designs. New creations by artist makers are also very popular now.

GOLLY GIRL
This charming golly girl, c.1910, is extremely rare and was bought and probably made in the USA. She is stuffed with wood wool and has a protruding nose. Her eyes are white cardboard circles with black boot buttons in the centre, her mouth is red stitching and her hair is made of wool. She is wearing handstitched long white pantaloons and a petticoat, while her cotton dress is trimmed with velvet ribbon and lace. All these clothes are original, which adds to her value.
Ht 56cm (22in),
£800–1,000 ($1,200–1,500)

HOMEMADE GOLLY WITH GOLLY CUP AND SAUCER
Golly china is very collectable – this English cup and saucer, c.1915, depicts a golly and wooden doll. Homemade golly dolls, on the other hand, can be found quite cheaply. The important thing is to get them in good, clean condition. Dating from 1955, this golly's body and face are made from black synthetic fabric. **Cup and saucer: £150–175 ($225–262). Golly: ht 51cm (20in), £30–50 ($45–75)**

MERRYTHOUGHT GOLLY
This 1950s golly was probably made by Merrythought, although it has no label to prove it. He is made in black felt and his hair is plush. His face has a centre seam and his clear glass eyes have black pupils and are backed with circles of white felt. His nostrils are stitched with white silk and the smiling mouth is made of red felt. **Ht 41cm (16in), £100–200 ($150–300)**

STEIFF GOLLY
This very rare Steiff golly is unusual because, rather than the more common long red trousers, he is wearing leather boots over his felt legs. Steiff made its first golly in 1908 and it remained in production until about 1917. This golly, c.1912, is fully jointed, his clothes are made of felt and he has the early protruding nose. **Ht 33cm (13in), £12,000–15,000 ($18,000–22,500)**

BOOK AND GOLLY DOLL
This is the first book by Florence Upton. Although she wrote more, the Dutch dolls did not appear on the covers again as it was the "golliwogg" who had become the main attraction. The golly doll, c.1920, on the right has white rabbit fur hair, a painted moulded face and fabric trousers. **Book: £250–350 ($375–525). Golly: ht 14cm (5½in), £100–120 ($150–180)**

GOLLIES

GOLLY AND PLAYING CARDS
The card game, made in London c.1900, depicts a golly doll and wooden dolls based on Florence Upton's designs. The large 1950s golly has plastic eyes and a red felt mouth. He is dressed in a yellow waistcoat and striped trousers and is very similar to Merrythought gollies, but he has no identifying label.
**Cards: £80–100 ($120–150).
Golly: ht 41cm (16in),
£100–125 ($150–190)**

MERRYTHOUGHT GOLLY
Condition alters the value of gollies a lot because they are difficult to restore. This example, c.1964, is pristine and even has his original foot label. He also has musical chimes in his body. His striped trousers are cotton and his jacket is velour. He has plastic eyes and synthetic hair, which is typical of later gollies. **Ht 36cm (14in), £200–300 ($300–450)**

PLATE, BOX & SCENT BOTTLES
These bottles contained perfume called "Le Golliwogg", which was made between 1920 and 1930 by Vigny of Paris. The bottles were originally presented in satin-lined boxes. The golly heads on the top of each one have seal skin hair. The painted plate was made in England in the 1950s and the small box, c.1920, was used to hold powder. The pieces range in value from £100 to £200 ($150 to $300).

WENDY BOSTON GOLLY

Made c.1965, this golly has the typical face of those produced by Wendy Boston. He has white eyebrows, round eyes and a smiling mouth, all printed on his cotton face. This golly was very simply made as an all-in-one piece, with non-removable clothes and foam stuffing. He has pantaloon-style trousers but, unusually for a golly, no separate jacket. Ht 30cm (12in), £40–50 ($60–75)

DEAN'S GOLLY

This golly, c.1960, has a yellow Dean's Gwentoy label sewn in the back seam of his body (see p.31). He is foam stuffed, and his printed cotton body is covered by a removable blue felt jacket. His facial features have been printed on and his hair is synthetic plush. He also has charming, sideways-glancing black plastic eyes. Ht 41cm (16in), £40–50 ($60–75)

CHAD VALLEY GOLLY WITH BUCKET

This golly, c.1955, has the typical features of the gollies that were made in England during the 1950s and '60s – plush hair, plastic eyes and a red nose and mouth. The yellow waistcoat is also common on English gollies and his red jacket is removable. The child's bucket is a contemporary addition as a prop. Ht 38cm (15in), £60–80 ($90–120)

CHAD VALLEY GOLLY

This Chad Valley golly, c.1960, is in mint condition and still has his card label, which is very rare. The blue and white label on his side seam says "Chad Valley Hygienic Toys". His face is black cotton and the features have been stuck on, while his hair is plush. The red and white striped trousers, yellow waistcoat with red buttons and blue jacket are all typical of the clothing found on Chad Valley gollies. Ht 41cm (16in), £100–150 ($150–225)

BEARS' FRIENDS – STEIFF

• Very early animals, c.1900, were made in felt and velvet. They were unjointed and had black bead or shoe-button eyes.

• Early pull-along animals had metal wheels but in c.1915 wooden wheels were introduced.

• During the 1920s and '30s many animals were made of mohair and had glass eyes.

• Some animals have mechanisms to give them realistic movements, such as the eccentric wheel and ball-jointed necks.

• After World War II, animals were made in synthetic fabrics and given plastic eyes.

Margarete Steiff made her first toy, a felt elephant, from a magazine pattern in 1880, and very soon she was making a whole range of different animals. These early, unjointed animals were featured in the Steiff catalogue for 1882. They included pull-along toys on metal wheels, skittle sets, Roly Poly animals and rattles made of felt plush and velvet. Birds, as well as a wide variety of both domestic and wild animals, were included. Dogs were particularly popular and most breeds were represented at some point. In the 1920s they actually became the company's bestselling items. Many were sold as adult toys and were carried as fashion accessories. Animals continued to be made, and in the 1950s a whole range was created in new synthetic fabric as well as in more traditional mohair. Such animals' popularity has continued throughout Steiff's history, right up to the present day.

DRESSED ELEPHANT
Steiff made a series of standing dressed animals that had soft fabric bodies underneath their clothes and their head and arms were made in mohair. The range included dogs, cats, bears and ducks and many were dressed in Bavarian clothes. This elephant, c.1939, is shown here with a woolly bird from the 1950s. The elephant is particularly desirable to collectors because he is in his original, pristine condition.
Ht 28cm (11in), £800–1,000 ($1,200–1,500)

TUMBLING ELEPHANT

This rare elephant, c.1909, is activated by winding one of the arms in a clockwork direction like a key. This winds the mechanism inside the animal to enable it to somersault. He is made in mohair and is fully jointed. The elephant was introduced in 1909, along with a somersaulting bear, a monkey and an Eskimo doll. **Ht 23cm (9in), £1,200–1,500 ($1,800–2,250)**

A RANGE OF ANIMALS

In 1903 some of the animals were given string jointing for the first time – along with the bears. They also received the elephant button in the ear. From 1905 they became disc jointed and had the printed button. Franz Steiff, a nephew of Margarete, then designed a new ball-jointed mechanism for realistic movable heads in 1908, which was used on polar bears, pigs and a begging poodle.

In 1912 Record Peter was introduced – a monkey on a chassis of metal with four wooden wheels that could be moved. He was a great success and was produced up until the 1950s. A great range of animals and birds was also then put on eccentric wooden wheels that gave them naturalistic movements. In 1930, for example, a dog called Rattler was fitted with a mechanism that moved his head when the tail was turned. This was particularly successful and other animals were fitted with the movement as a result.

LION PINCUSHION

This pincushion , c.1913, is made in green velvet and edged with silk cord but unfortunately it is now very worn. The lion has a velvet body and face and the mane is mohair. He has black shoe-button eyes. **Ht 18cm (7in), £1,200–1,500 ($1,800–2,250)**

THREE POLAR BEARS

These polar bears are made in mohair and have jointed limbs. The range comes in five sizes; the larger two here are c.1910 and the central one is c.1909. Their ball-jointed necks enable their heads to rotate in a realistic manner. The navy jacket on the smallest bear is not original. **Left and right: ht 33cm (13in), £1,000–1,200 ($1,500–1,800). Centre: ht 22cm (8½in), £700–900 ($1,050–1,350)**

TWO MAMMOTHS

Mammoths such as the two shown here were made from 1909 to 1920 and came in felt or mohair. These unjointed examples, c.1915, are made of mohair and are in original condition. The red mammoth is rather worn, which does lower his value, but his long tusks are still present. These animals are not seen very often and are therefore highly collectable. **Left: ht 20cm (8in), £300 ($450). Right: ht 13cm (5in), £800 ($1,200)**

BEARS' FRIENDS – STEIFF

BULLY DOG
This rare large Steiff Bully dog, made c.1932, has his original leather collar, trimmed with horsehair and studded with 13 Steiff buttons. He has a swivel head and large, wired, posable ears. His light-coloured facemask is made of velvet, he has an embroidered nose and large brown and black glass eyes. The rest of his head and body is made of mohair and stuffed with wood wool. **Ht 50cm (20in), £2,000–2,500 ($3,000–3,750)**

STEIFF DACHSHUND
This comical dachshund is very rare and therefore highly collectable. He has an elephant button in his ear and black button eyes. He is un-jointed, made of velvet and stuffed with wood wool. He is recorded as one of the newest novelties at the 1903 and 1904 Leipzig Fairs on a photograph that was taken at the time. **Length 30cm (12in), £800–1,000 ($1,200–1,500)**

FLUFFY THE CAT
Fluffy the Cat was introduced in a sitting position in 1926. The label with the metal edge that can be seen on the larger cat was used from 1926 to 1928. Fluffy is made in tipped mohair and has large glass eyes. She was produced until just after World War II. **Left: ht 13cm (5in), £700–800 ($1,050–1,200). Right: ht 8cm (3in), £300–500 ($450–750)**

STEIFF MOUSE
Early Steiff mice were often sold as a set together with a cat, but also came individually. This one, c.1905, has black button eyes and is rather worn. **Ht 5cm (2in), £200–300 ($300–450)**

TWO EARLY STEIFF CATS
The velvet cat on the left, c.1905, has green glass eyes and contains a rattle. He is in a very worn state, which decreases his value somewhat. The rare, early velvet Roly Poly cat on the right, c.1900, is on a wooden base. He was made before metal buttons were used in the ears. Steiff Roly Poly animals were first made in 1898 and the range also included bears (*see* p.87). **Left: 13cm (5in), £200–300 ($300–450). Right: 13cm (5in), £800–1,200 ($1,200–1,800)**

TOM CAT
Black cats were first made in 1903 and over the years the design has changed. The version made in the late 1920s, for example, was of velvet with a mohair tail, but the Tom Cat shown here, c.1955, is all mohair, with a long fluffy tail. This type was made from 1950 to 1976, is unjointed and has an arched back. This one also has green glass eyes and whiskers. His pink ribbon is original but he is missing his chest label. **Ht 15cm (6in), £100–150 ($150–225)**

PUCK THE GNOME WITH PIGS
Puck the Gnome is made of linen but his clothes and face are felt. This example is c.1914. The begging pig on the left, c.1910, is very unusual. He would originally have been wearing a felt jacket. The unjointed pig on the right, c.1920, is made of mohair. **Left: ht 20cm (8in), £800–1,200 ($1,200–1,800). Centre and right: ht/length 36cm (14in), £500–700 ($750–1,050) each**

BEARS' FRIENDS – PANDAS

IDENTIFYING FEATURE

This Merrythought label dates from the 1930s. It was used until 1957, when "Hygienic Toys" was replaced with "Ironbridge Shrops".

MERRYTHOUGHT PANDA

This panda is made in mohair and is fully jointed. He has felt pads with a label on his right paw, his eyes are glass and his head is quite large. Merrythought was one of the earliest manufacturers to produce a soft toy panda. In their catalogue for 1937 they offered two designs: one was a realistic panda standing on all fours and the other a panda teddy bear made in black and white mohair. This example is c.1938. **Ht 53cm (21in), £200–300 ($300–450)**

TWO STEIFF PANDAS

These two Steiff pandas are both made of mohair and are c.1955. They have straight legs and large flat feet that enable them to stand upright. Their arms are also straight and have downward-facing paw pads. Their distinctive open mouths are lined with felt and they have glass eyes. The panda on the right is especially desirable because he still retains his chest tag and the button in his ear. **Left: ht 28cm (11in), £600–700 ($900–1,050). Right: ht 23cm (9in), £400–500 ($600–750)**

THE APPEAL OF PANDAS

The panda is one of the rarest animals on earth and is now a fully protected, endangered species. In the late 1930s the first pandas arrived in Western zoos – in 1938 London Zoo received two adult pandas and a female seven-month-old baby called Ming. These pandas caused a sensation as the public were enthralled with the black and white, furry, bear-like animals. It did not take long for the toy manufacturers to realize that the panda would make a very delightful soft toy. Shops were quickly filled with panda bears and novelties of every kind. Dean's Rag Book Co. even went so far as to have their Panda, "Handy Pandy", photographed with Ming in her cage. Tara Toys, the Irish makers, made pandas from the late 1940s, while Chad Valley and Chiltern produced their own in the '50s. In 1953 Schuco added a Tricky Yes/No panda to their teddy range. Pandas are still loved today and continue to be made by both manufacturers and artists; the designs vary quite considerably between makers, as some look far more realistic than others.

RED-PAWED PANDA
This panda is probably by Chad Valley and he is c.1960. He is made in very short black and white mohair, his body is chubby and hard stuffed with wood wool and he also has a squeaker. His head is large and his face quite flat. His short, straight arms have red rexine paw pads at their ends, as do the feet. **Ht 51cm (20in), £100–200 ($150–300)**

CHILTERN PANDA
This panda, c.1950, is made to the same pattern as the Hugmee bear of the 1950s and has all the same features – brown and black glass eyes, a vertically stitched, shield-shaped nose and cupped ears sewn into the facial seam. The velvet paw pads have four claw stitches sewn in pairs across the pad. **Ht 41cm (16in), £200–300 ($300–450)**

PAIR OF CHILTERN PANDAS
The large panda, c.1950, is made in mohair and has oversized black patches round his eyes. The smaller panda, c.1963, has a label sewn into the side seam and is made in cotton plush. His black plastic nose is a typical Chiltern feature of the 1960s. **Left: ht 38cm (15in), £200–300 ($300–450). Right: ht 30cm (12in), £100–200 ($150–300)**

OTHER BEARS' FRIENDS

OOLOO THE CAT
Ooloo the Cat was made by Chad Valley and it is very rare indeed to find one today, particularly in such good original condition. This 1930 example is made in velvet and has unusual glass eyes. Ooloo was created by the artist George Study as a successor for Bonzo the Dog and she appeared in a cartoon in *The Daily Sketch* newspaper in 1922. **Ht 24cm (9½in), £800–900 ($1,200–1,350)**

MUSICAL CAT
This is a 1925 musical cat with a Helvetic squeeze-type musical box in his tummy. He also has wonderful long, silky mohair that is still in excellent condition. He has his original yellow eyes too, as well as the pink silk mouth and horizontal nose stitching. Cats like this are very popular with collectors today. **Ht 23cm (9in), £600–700 ($900–1,050)**

TWO MONKEYS
The green mohair monkey on the left was made by Alpha Farnell in 1930. He has a felt face and ears, is wearing earrings and is smoking a cigarette. The monkey on the right is a 1925 Schuco Yes/No, made in red mohair with felt paws and feet. Monkeys were very popular in the 1920s and '30s. **Left: ht 30cm (12in). Right: ht 20cm (8in). Both £300–400 ($450–600)**

SKATER RABBIT

This skater rabbit was made by Chiltern in the early 1930s and is in great, unfaded condition. She is made of mohair and her pink jacket and muff is sewn onto her body. She is unjointed and was designed to stand up, so her feet are flat. Chiltern also made a skater bear in artificial silk plush, which was dressed exactly the same except for a pill-box hat on her head. **Ht 28cm (11in), £600–700 ($900–1,050)**

FARNELL ELEPHANT

This 1930 elephant has the Alpha Farnell label still on his foot and is a very unusual example of their work because he stands up, again aided by flat feet. This particular elephant has a head made of mohair while his clothes are felt and fully removable. He has glass eyes, felt tusks and an open mouth lined with red felt, while his shoes are made of rexine. Steiff also made a standing elephant around that time, which can be confused with Farnell's. **Ht 30cm (12in), £400–500 ($600–750)**

DOG-ON-WHEELS

Made by Chiltern in 1962, this dog-on-wheels still retains its original label. It is made of mohair and has a black plastic nose. Chiltern made a wide range of these toys on wheels. **Ht 51cm (20in), £50–80 ($75–120)**

TWO SCHUCO MONKEYS

Both these monkeys are from 1950. The monkey on the left is a rare Yes/No orang-utan, which are highly sought after today. The Schuco Yes/No Tricky monkey on the right still retains his plastic ID tag, which is sewn under his jacket. His clothes are all original. **Left: ht 46cm (18in), £800–900 ($1,200–1,350). Right: ht 30cm (12in), £350–450 ($525–675)**

CHAD VALLEY DOG & RABBIT

The Roly Poly rabbit was made by Chad Valley in 1965 from red and white synthetic plush. The dog retains his original 1970 card label with the words "Chad Valley Chiltern" on it, and he also has a printed label sewn into the seam of his leg. He is made in synthetic plush and is washable. He was made at Chiltern after Chad Valley's takeover in 1967. **Left: ht 15cm (6in), £30–50 ($45–75). Right: ht 20cm (8in), £40–50 ($60–75)**

CHARACTER BEARS

DISPLAYING CHARACTER BEARS

This collection of little characters, of varying vintages and styles, is displayed in an old doll's bathroom complete with a plastic duck!

This little character bear sits in a battered child's suitcase, surrounded by old toys and two miniature newspapers of the period.

Character bears can be very appealing and have an irresistible charm all their own for many collectors, either as a part of a hug dotted among more pristine bears, or as a collection in their own right. But what is a character bear? They are usually relatively inexpensive, as condition is not important; in fact saggy stuffing, missing eyes, balding fur, old restoration such as altered paw pads and the odd patch here and there, all gained through many years of love and affection, are part of their character. Often the identity of the manufacturer is unknown but in the case of character bears many collectors find this of little significance. Clothing and accessories are an important part of character bears – some of these will be old family bits and pieces (a knitted sweater, an old school cap, a child's pyjamas) cut down to fit. It is wonderful if you can find these old characters in original condition, but it is not easy. Instead you might decide to find an old battered ted and create your own little character bear.

GROUP OF CHARACTER BEARS
The Chiltern bear on the left, with the red and cream striped sweater, is in good condition, unlike the little character sitting in front of him with his blue eyes, battered nose and large patch sewn across the top of his head. The old blue bear on the right is very faded and worn and his ears are lopsided, but in his oversized old red jacket he is a real character.

NIGHT-TIME BEARS
Using a theme for dressing or grouping character bears can be very effective. These three bears are all ready for bed, clothed in children's pyjamas and dressing gowns. The sweet little girl bear on the right is in an old nightdress. Her paw pads have been restored using some very unusual striped cotton material, and she is missing the stitching from her mouth, giving her a rather quirky appearance.

BEAR FRIENDS

Putting large and small character bears together makes a charming display. The large bear is a great character, with her floppy head and droopy ears. Her mohair is very sparse, she has hardly any nose stitching at all and she has odd pads on her feet. The bears sitting in her lap are an old Chad Valley and a tiny bear with an old blue jacket pinned by a badge.

SCHOOLBOY CHARACTER

This wonderful old bear has seen better days – he is missing one eye, his stuffing is showing through and his nose has been patched – but he looks very jaunty sitting on his Victorian rocking chair, with his cricket cap on his head covered in badges. He is wearing an old school tie and sweater that once belonged to his original owner.

WELL-WORN CHARACTERS

These three bears are all showing signs of having been well loved. The largest character has rather sparse mohair, covered by a blue knitted dress and shoes and a restitched nose. The bear on the right has a very sweet face and is suitably adorned in a pretty print dress. The smallest character bear has had his nose worn away completely by too many cuddles.

AMERICAN CHARACTER BEAR

This bear was bought in the USA and came complete with his wonderful collection of brooches and badges. He has befriended a small English rabbit by his side. He is probably an Ideal bear from the 1920s and is in very good condition, proving that not all characters are tatty. There are no hard and fast rules as to what a character bear should be like – it is really down to the individual collector.

LADY BEAR WITH HER PEKE

This lady has great style. She is very bald and her original eyes have gone, but with a feathered hat, replacement button eyes and a velvet coat that probably came from an antique doll, she retains her charm. The Pekingese dog was made by Steiff. Such a delightful bear would appeal to any collector.

BEAR MEMORABILIA

When collecting bears it is not necessary to be limited purely to the stuffed toy teddy bear, as there is a wide variety of other objects. Many of these pieces were modelled on real bears, especially those that were made during the19th century, before the advent of the teddy bear. At that time performing bears were very popular and so were often depicted on china, silver and pottery. At the turn of the century, carved wooden bears known as Black Forest bears were produced in all sorts of forms, including desk and smoking accessories. There were also items produced that were meant for babies, such as rattles and teething rings, which were modelled on the cuter, soft teddy bear of 1908. In the 1900s bears became the subject of fashion accessories and their images were used on silver brooches, hatpins and earrings. Children's china throughout the years has often been decorated with bears – dolls' tea sets and baby dishes and mugs are particularly worth looking out for. It is often possible to find these pieces of memorabilia at boot fairs and flea markets.

CUCKOO CLOCK
This very rare Black Forest figural bear cuckoo clock is made in carved wood. When the hands of the clock reach the top at the start of each new hour the doors open and the cuckoo sings. The carving on this piece is of a very high quality, indicating it was probably made in Switzerland, c.1915.
Ht 61cm (24in), £2,000–2,500 ($3,000–3,750)

BEAR BELL
This Black Forest bear, c.1900, is carved out of wood and stands on a metal dinner bell. Despite their name, such bears were mostly carved in Switzerland, rather than in the Black Forest in Germany. **Ht 16.5cm (6½in), £200–250 ($300–375)**

INKWELL AND PEN

This Black Forest carved inkwell, c.1912, is highly detailed and depicts a bear sitting on a tree trunk. The bear tips back to reveal an inkwell; he is holding a most unusual bear nib-pen that has a metal base and a carved wooden top. Unusual and detailed pieces such as this are highly sought after by collectors but are not easily found. Inkwell: ht 20cm (8in), £200–250 ($300–375). Pen: £30–40 ($45–60)

THE POPULAR & UNUSUAL

Bear memorabilia offers today's collector a wealth of items in every price range imaginable. While early pieces can often be extremely expensive, bears have in fact been used to decorate items right up to the present day and some of the newer pieces can be found and bought quite cheaply. Teddy bear jewellery is one of the most popular and easily collected areas – for example, you will find gold and silver charms for bracelets, earrings, pendants, costume jewellery and even rings with bear themes to them. There are also some particularly unusual items out there waiting to be discovered and snapped up by collectors. Indeed, bears have appeared in the form of soaps, hot-water bottles and even golf club covers to name just a few. There is a lot of fun to be had hunting out such rare teddy bear memorabilia, both antique and modern, and don't forget that it will also add another dimension to your collection as a whole.

BEAR GREASE JARS

These very unusual ceramic jars are both c.1890 and are still in excellent condition. Jars such as these fall into two collecting categories, as they appeal to collectors of pots and boxes, as well as to those looking for bear memorabilia. Left: diam. 6cm (2½in), £125–150 ($190–225). Right: diam. 9cm (3½in), £50–70 ($75–105)

BEAR BRUSH & CORK STOPPER

Carved bears, such as these two examples, c.1912, were made as souvenirs and often carry the name of a town in Switzerland or Germany. The brush on the left was probably for removing crumbs from a tablecloth and the stopper was for use in a wine bottle. Left: ht 13cm (5in), £60–80 ($90–120). Right: ht 11.5cm (4½in), £70–80 ($105–120)

INKWELL AND TOBACCO JAR

A Russian maker called Lomanosov made the unusual china inkwell and pen rest, c.1930, pictured below left. The top of the tree trunk lifts off to reveal the white milk glass ink pot. The Majolica-ware figural bear tobacco jar is c.1912. Here it is the head of the bear that lifts off to reveal where the tobacco is kept. Left: ht 15cm (6in), £225–250 ($340–375). Right: ht 23cm (9in), £300–380 ($450–570)

BEAR MEMORABILIA

PHOTO ALBUM

This Victorian photo album is a rare item indeed. It has an elaborate cover made of celluloid, a green lacy border and a metal clasp. Because it was made c.1890, before the advent of the teddy bear, the image depicts real bears. The picture is of a Victorian lady riding in a sleigh drawn by a team of bears, while Cupid sits on her shoulder whipping the bears on. **Ht 26.5cm (10½in), £125–150 ($190–225)**

HATPIN HOLDER AND POCKET WATCH HOLDER

The brass hatpin holder, c.1900, contains two hatpins, c.1910 and 1920. Both pins are sterling silver; the left bear has ruby-red glass eyes, and the other is a flip-top bear. The pocket watch holder is c.1900 and made of pewter. **Left: ht 15cm (6in), £425–550 ($640–825). Right: ht12.5cm (5in), £150–175 ($225–260)**

CIGAR CUTTER AND CARD HOLDER

On the left is an unusual, c.1870, bronze bear cigar cutter. To the right is a silver-plated figural calling or business card holder made c.1915, etched with a picture of a polar bear on an ice slab. **Left: ht 16.5cm (6½in), £150–175 ($225–260). Right: ht 6cm (2½in), £60–80 ($90–120)**

TEDDY SOAPS

This unusual set of soap teddy bears playing cards at a table, c.1947, is in mint condition. The accompanying box is entitled "Four No Trump" and the set was made by Lightfoot of New York, who also created the "Toboggan Teddies". Toiletries were often made depicting teddy bears at this time. **Ht 10cm (4in), £60–70 ($90–105)**

RATTLE & HOT-WATER BOTTLE

On the left is a yellow celluloid teddy bear baby rattle on a wire frame, c.1930. It has no identifying marks but most were made in Japan. The American red rubber child's hot-water bottle, c.1935, still retains its original black Bakelite stopper. It has "Teddy" written on the back. **Left: ht 18cm (7in), £10–15 ($15–22). Right: ht 30cm (12in), £30–35 ($45–52)**

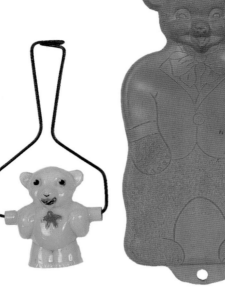

SILVER BABY ITEMS

This range of silver items includes a food pusher on the far left, two spoons and two rattles. Their heights vary from 6cm (2½in) to 16.5cm (6½in). They are all from the early 1900s and all English, except for the food pusher which is American. Such items may include ivory details, like the rattle on the left, while others are engraved. **Values range from £50 to 300 ($75 to 450); the silver and ivory rattle is the dearest.**

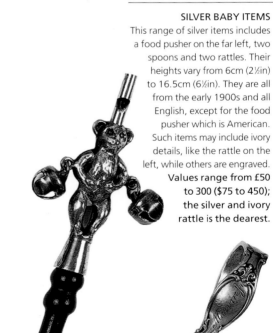

ADVERTISING & EPHEMERA

ADVERTISING GIMMICKS

This American trade card for Lion's Coffee was one of a set from 1907 depicting Goldilocks and the Three Bears, given away with each purchase.

The image of the bear was used in advertising long before the stuffed toy teddy bear was created in 1903, but the teddy bear soon caught the public's imagination. Manufacturers used the image to promote all manner of products, from chocolates to hosiery, cereals to brandy, and the shape of the teddy altered over the years to reflect the changing bear designs from the 1900s to the present day. Sometimes a bear may be drawn realistically, or standing on his hind legs engaging in human activities, and often humorously and mischievously. Collecting sheet music with "teddy bear" in the title is popular – there are teddy bear waltzes, teddy bear marches and the all-time favourite *Teddy Bears' Picnic*, first broadcast on BBC Radio in the 1930s. Sheet music often has colourful graphics of bears on the cover and these are also very collectable. Postcards featuring bears can be fascinating and affordable and are easy to display. Popular during the teddy bear craze of the early 1900s, they were often sent from seaside resorts, or as greetings cards. They can be found at specialist fairs and flea markets.

ROWNTREES ADVERTISEMENT
This charming teddy bear, c.1925, is made of cardboard and is free-standing. Advertising the famous sweet-manufacturers Rowntrees, it shows the teddy bear striding out carrying a banner with the words "Rowntrees Chocolates In Fancy Boxes". The company still produces sweets today. This is an unusual item and would be a nice addition to any teddy bear collection. **Ht: 60cm (24in), £80–90 ($120–135)**

COGNAC ADVERT
This advertising piece, c.1910, is printed on tin and shows a bear as a waiter serving a bottle of brandy on a silver tray with the words "Coming Sir". Two cases of the brandy are on the floor behind him. This is in fact an American advert for a French brandy. **Ht: 66cm (26in), £150–250 ($225–375)**

SANTA AND THE BEARS

These three cards, which join to make the full picture as shown, were given away separately with subscriptions to a paper published by Western Newspapers in the USA. The picture shows Santa with a sleigh full of toys, whipping a team of bears forward through the forest, watched by reindeer. It was painted c.1907 by Frank Verbeck – a well-known artist who drew a series of these bear pictures. Ht 25.5cm (10in), £80–90 ($120–135)

TEDDY SHEET MUSIC

These two pieces of sheet music both feature bears. On the left is *Teddy Bear Pieces* by J.S. Fearis, published by McKinley Music of Chicago c.1920. *The Big Brown Bear* on the right is a piano piece, c.1930, called a "dance grotesque". The cover is very simple, making it less valuable than those with more detailed bear graphics. **Left: £25–30 ($40–45). Right: £10–15 ($15–20)**

TEDDY BEAR POSTCARDS

The postcard on the left, c.1930, is typical of the type that carried a greeting; it has a play on words – "Bearing your birthday in mind". The picture is drawn and signed by an artist. The card on the right is a more simple drawing, again featuring a play on words, and dating from 1950. **Ht: both 15cm (6in). Left: £20–25 ($30–40). Right: £15–20 ($20–30)**

PRIMLEY GUM ADVERT

This advertisement for Primley's California Fruit Chewing Gum appeared in *Leslie's Weekly Ladies' Magazine* of 1894. This is an early piece of advertising portraying real bears rather than teddy bears. Bears were used extensively in the late 19th century for advertising – they were seen as cuddly, jolly and often naughty animals. Here a mother bear and her cubs have opened a box of Primley's Chewing Gum and are eating the contents. **Ht: 41cm (16in), £20–30 ($30–45)**

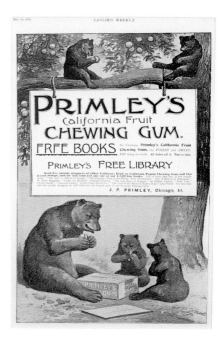

ADVERTISING BEAR

This teddy bear, c.1912, is a rare item as he carries an advertisement on his body. He is made of rather poor-quality short bristle mohair. Set into his back is a square piece of cotton with the words "Bear Brand Genuine Swiss Milk" with a faded logo in the middle. This most likely refers to Swiss milk chocolate. **Ht: 25cm (10in), £400–500 ($600–750)**

STAR BEARS

There are many bears with star quality but some bears have become so famous that they are now recognized in many countries around the world and written about in many different languages. Often originating from a book or cartoon, such is their popularity that they are soon transferred into the more starry world of film and television. When Walt Disney bought the rights to Winnie-the-Pooh in 1964, he catapulted the shy, honey-loving bear into superstardom by giving him his own animated motion picture, which was screened in 1966. Soon Pooh and his friends were as well known and loved as Disney's own creation, Mickey Mouse, who first appeared in 1928. Many of the principal manufacturers of teddy bears in the USA and also in Europe made versions of these and other famous characters. As well as looking for the bears themselves, it is fun to collect the myriad of merchandise that resulted from the films and TV programmes, including books, puzzles, toys and games. Shown here are just some of the many star bears that have reached out and touched the lives of adults and children alike.

WINNIE-THE-POOH AND PIGLET
This Pooh bear is by American maker Agnes Brush, made c.1952 with the permission of Steven Slesinger Inc. who held the copyright from Milne until Disney bought it in 1964. He is made of tan flannel with shoe-button eyes; his red sweater is not original. Piglet is a sample bear made by Gund, c.1964. **Pooh: ht 33cm (13in), £200–250 ($300–375). Piglet: ht 25cm (10in), £50–60 ($75–90)**

MERRYTHOUGHT KANGA AND ROO AND PIGLET
The Kanga and Roo toys are made of mohair (Roo fits into Kanga's pouch) and Piglet is made in pink velveteen. They are all c.1970. Together with Eeyore and Pooh they form a set made by Merrythought from 1966. The design of the characters is based on the Disney cartoon film of 1966, not the original Ernest Shepard drawings. **Piglet: ht 23cm (9in), £100–150 ($150–225). Kanga & Roo: ht 41cm (16in), £150–200 ($225–300)**

MERRYTHOUGHT BEAR AND BOOK

This bear by Merrythought was made c.1935. He has a button in his ear and is wearing a red sweater to make him look like Winnie-the-Pooh. The book is very interesting: it is entitled *Winnie Ille Pu* and is the Latin version of Milne's story, translated by a Hungarian doctor called Alexander Lenard in 1960. It became the first book in Latin to make the New York bestsellers list. **Bear: ht 38cm (15in), £400–450 ($600–675)**

LIMITED EDITIONS

These two books are a limited edition box set, one of 250 published in London in 1928. The one on the right is signed by A.A. Milne and Ernest Shepard (*see* opposite), which greatly

increases its value. *Winnie-the-Pooh* was first published in London in 1926, and in New York two weeks later, and was the first book to feature Pooh as the main character. **Left: £800–900 ($1,200–1,350). Right: £2,000–2,200 ($3,000–3,300)**

BEARS IN THE LIMELIGHT

There are other bears that have become stars, though not perhaps as globally as Pooh or Mickey Mouse. One such bear is Paddington, who is named after the train station in London. The original bear on whom he was based was bought by Michael Bond as a Christmas present for his wife and Bond was inspired to write a story about the little brown bear, with his battered suitcase and jar of marmalade. The resulting book, *A Bear called Paddington*, was published in 1958 and Bond went on to write 26 more books. Paddington soon had his own animated television programme, and soft-toy versions of Paddington and his Aunt Lucy were manufactured by an English toy company called Gabrielle Designs.

Sooty and Sweep were simple glove puppets operated by Harry Corbett and they first appeared on British TV in 1952. Their antics and conjuring tricks were such a success that they were given their own TV series, which became one of the longest-ever running children's shows.

A bear with completely different star quality is Smokey Bear, who is famous all over the USA as a symbol of fire prevention and is known as "The Guardian of the Forest". He first appeared on a poster in the 1940s to launch a very successful forest fire prevention campaign and has since become a national figure and a symbol of conservation.

FREDDIE FARNELL

This fabulous Alpha Farnell bear, c.1930, appeared on the BBC's *Antiques Roadshow* in 1999 and is owned by Sue Pearson herself. He had been wrapped up for many years in a wardrobe and when the antiques expert revealed the high value of the bear, the original owner decided to sell him at auction. Freddie was the star of the sale and appeared on the television news the same evening. **Ht 66cm (26in), £4,000–4,500 ($6,000–6,750)**

MICKEY AND MINNIE MOUSE BY DEANS.

The larger figures, c.1935, are very rare and were probably showroom models. Made of velveteen and felt, they are in perfect condition, complete with their tails which are often missing. The small Mickey and Minnie, c.1934, with their large flat hands, are of a size more commonly found. **Back: Mickey ht 76cm (30in), Minnie ht 63.5cm (25in), £2,000–2,500 ($3,000–3,750) each. Front pair: ht 19cm (7½in), £300–350 ($450–525) each**

STAR BEARS

SOOTY COLLECTING BOX

This large papier-mâché charity collecting box was made c.1960 for the Royal National Institute for the Blind. It shows Sooty bear holding the collecting box and his famous wand, which featured in his magician's act. It is a measure of Sooty's popularity during the 1950s and '60s that his image was used in this way. **Ht 91.5cm (36in), £100–150 ($150–225)**

CHAD VALLEY GLOVE PUPPETS

These two glove puppets, c.1960, show Sooty with his friend Sweep, the spaniel-type dog that joined him on his TV show in 1955. Together they created havoc for Harry Corbett, who was always the victim, and delighted their TV audience. Soo the panda arrived on the scene in 1962 and was the first of the characters to speak; Harry's wife Marjory provided her voice. **Both: ht 25cm (10in), £100–150 ($150–225) the pair**

SOOTY GAMES AND NOVELTIES

Collectors of Sooty can find a wide variety of games and novelties such as these, dating from the 1960s. Sooty's first TV series was called *Sooty the Teddy Bear Magician*. At the end of every show Sooty played *Teddy Bear's Picnic* on a xylophone. Various companies manufactured the Sooty xylophone, but it was Chad Valley that held the rights to the glove puppets for many years. They also made the game of tiddleywinks pictured. Eventually other companies made Sooty merchandise. **£30–75 ($45–115)**

AUNT LUCY

Aunt Lucy was manufactured by Gabrielle and is much harder to find than Paddington. She is hard stuffed, enabling her to stand alone; this example, c.1981, is in excellent condition. Aunt Lucy came to pay Paddington a visit from her home in "darkest Peru" in Bond's stories. She prefers boiled sweets to marmalade! Ht 40.5cm (16in), £100–160 ($150–240)

EDEN TOYS PADDINGTON AND GABRIELLE GLOVE PUPPET

Eden Toys in the USA have produced Paddington since 1975 and this example was made c.1980. He differs from the original, created by Gabrielle Designs, as he is not wearing Paddington's famous red Wellington boots. The rare glove puppet, c.1985, is by Gabrielle Designs, who made the first ever version. **Bear: ht 35.5cm (14in), £30–40 ($45–60). Puppet: 20cm (8in), £40–50 ($60–75)**

SMOKEY BEAR

This example of Smokey Bear was made by R. Dakin and Co., c.1970. He is made of plastic with movable arms and his denim trousers are removable. Dakin also produced a plush version. Smokey is made under licence from the "Cooperative Fire Prevention Program". Ht 38cm (15in), £30–40 ($45–60)

NOOKIE BEAR

Roger de Courcey and his ventriloquist's bear, Nookie, first appeared on TV in 1976 and proved to be a big hit. Since then Nookie and Roger have become famous, appearing regularly on TV and several times at the London Palladium theatre. Nookie became a best-selling child's toy and this example, c.1970, is made in synthetic fabric and is fully jointed except for his head. Ht 51cm (20in), £100–150 ($150–225)

LITERARY BEARS

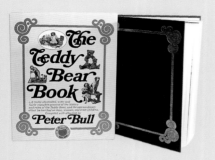

This is the House of Nisbit edition of Peter Bull's The Teddy Bear Book, *published in 1983 in a boxed limited edition of 10,000.*

This photo shows Peter Bull, the well-known actor, author and arctophile, with his bears Bully, Young Bully and Bully Minor.

The overwhelming success of the teddy bear on both sides of the Atlantic from the early part of the century gave rise to a great many children's books in which teddy bears featured very prominently. Other books focused on real bears having adventures, because real bears can stand upright and therefore be dressed and assume human characteristics. In the early 20th century, stories of Teddy B. and Teddy G., the Roosevelt bears, originated in the comic sections and supplements of the US Sunday newspapers. Paul Piper, who used the pen name Seymour Eaton, created them and his first book, published in the USA in 1906, was entitled *The Roosevelt Bears: Their Travels and Adventures.* He went on to write three more books, all in verse form and beautifully illustrated by four different artists. Another famous literary bear is Rupert, who first appeared in the *Daily Express* newspaper in 1920; books and annuals featuring Rupert and his friends in Nutwood village soon followed. Peter Bull, the actor and writer, possibly did more than anyone to inspire bear lovers everywhere, with his books and TV and radio appearances in the 1970s telling the stories of Bully Bear. There are limited editions to collect, as well as the memorabilia associated with these bears.

THREE NISBIT BEARS
The bear on the left is Bully Bear, created in 1981 by the House of Nisbit and inspired by Peter Bull's bear Delicatessen. The bear in the centre, c.1986, is Jack's Bear, named after Jack Wilson, chairman of Nisbit. The bear on the right, c.1987, is a replica of Delicatessen, Peter Bull's famous bear who played Aloysius in the BBC TV series *Brideshead Revisited*. **Left:** ht 46cm (18in), £80–100 ($120–150). **Centre:** ht 40.5cm (16in), £60–70 ($90–105). **Right:** ht 51cm (20in), £150–200 ($225–300).

TWO ROOSEVELT TIP TRAYS
The Roosevelt bears became so popular that many products carrying their image were made, such as these metal tip trays, c.1906, which were put on the counters of barber shops and tobacco stores for men to leave a tip. **£300–350 ($450–525) the pair**

REPLICA TEDDY B. AND TEDDY G.
These two replicas of the Roosevelt bears are a limited edition of 2,000 created by Dottie Ayers of The Calico Teddy Company, Baltimore, in 1999. The mohair bears are presented in a leather trunk, accompanied by a copy of the first Teddy B. and Teddy G. book by Seymour Eaton (see below). The B. and G. stand for brown and grey respectively. **Bears: ht 28cm (11in), £300 ($450) the set**

GROUP OF ROOSEVELT ITEMS.
These products are, from left to right: a silver baby spoon, c.1907, with the bears climbing the handle; a silver-plated match case, c.1906, with a picture of Teddy B; a stick pin, c.1905, also of Teddy B; and a Roosevelt bears postcard, c.1906. **Two silver items: £150–200 ($225–300). Stick pin: £75–80 ($115–120). Postcard: £20–40 ($30–60)**

RUPERT THE BEAR
Rupert Bear was created in 1920 by Mary Tourtel and became a well-known character in his check trousers, red sweater and yellow scarf. The stories of his adventures with his friends Bill Badger, Algy and Edward Trunk were very popular. Rupert Bear items like these are highly collectable. **Values range £12–30 ($18–45)**

ROOSEVELT BEARS BOOK AND MEMORABILIA
The book is a first edition of the Roosevelt Bears book written by Seymour Eaton in 1906. The tea cup and saucer were made by the Buffalo pottery company in 1905 and the milk-glass candy container is c.1906. **Book: £300–350 ($450–525). Cup and saucer: £100–150 ($150–225). Candy container: £200–250 ($300–375)**

LOOKING AFTER
YOUR BEARS

STEIFF SAILOR BEAR
This early Steiff bear, c.1908, has a fragile body that is well protected by his old sailor jacket. His long curly mohair must be brushed gently to keep him dust-free. **Ht: 36cm (24in),** £5,000–6,000 ($7,500–9,000)

CARE & RESTORATION

When you find the vintage bear of your dreams, the first thing to ask yourself is whether he needs restoration – unless of course you are actually lucky enough to find one in pristine condition. Sometimes very old bears have been handed down through several generations of one family and have spent the last years of their life in an attic or lying on top of a wardrobe. In such cases the years will have taken their toll – stuffing will probably have started to fall out and eyes may have been lost or taken out by mothers who were anxious about the safety of glass eyes held in place by metal wires. Moths view bears as sitting targets and see them as an especially good place to lay their eggs. Sticky children's fingers over the decades may have left mohair dull and dirty too. All these factors are worth considering when you find that all-important bear so it is best to take your time and have a good, long look at him to decide what needs doing. What follows is my own preferred method of care and restoration, gained from many years of experience. However, it is only intended as a guide, as every restorer has their own favourite way.

RESTORATION TIPS

Before you embark on any restoration, you should first identify the maker and approximate value of the bear. This is because you should not attempt any restoration on a rare or valuable bear yourself – always let an expert restorer do it for you. Once you have identified him, examine your bear's mohair, as light, heat and dust can all have a serious effect on teddies. Sunlight can fade the mohair but if you look inside the joints you can often see what the true colour is. There is no treatment to restore colour to mohair as you cannot tint it back successfully. Heat has the unfortunate effect of drying out mohair and making it brittle. This can be a particularly serious condition as the fabric may crumble when you attempt to sew it. Dust, on the other hand, makes the mohair dull and flat. This condition can be reversed by careful surface washing but do not immerse your teddy in water – see below for how to wash a bear. Remember to approach any restoration that you do yourself with caution. Do not attempt anything that is irreversible and if you are in doubt about anything then seek advice first. If you are considering buying an old bear that is in a fragile condition, remember that it can take a lot of time and patience to restore him back to his original state.

UNWELCOME VISITORS

Vintage bears that have become dusty and dirty over the years will probably have attracted moths and carpet beetles so you should give a bear a thorough check up for any signs of infestation, especially in joints and crevices. Felt paw pads are a moth's favourite lunch so look for the telltale signs of tiny holes and larvae husks that are found hidden among mohair – in extreme cases living larvae can be seen. If your bear has any of these symptoms then he must be treated

RESTORING PAW PADS ON EARLY BEARS

The following is a good method to employ when restoring paw pads on early bears. The original felt was able to be reused, but the cardboard inserts were damaged and had to be replaced by new cardboard. New German wool felt was stretched over these inserts and stitched into place and then the remains of the original felt was replaced over the new pads.

WORLD WAR I BEAR

This bear underwent extensive cleaning and restoration as he was in a very sorry state indeed. During the process he had to be opened up and inside was found an old newspaper from World War I. This was kept, as it is an interesting part of his history, and he was then restuffed using wood wool.

WHEN TO LEAVE PAWS ALONE
The feet on this Steiff bear are best left unrestored. The only work that was done was stitching the felt down to make it secure. Many early

Steiff bears had coloured felt lining in their paw pads, as the factory used any available felt. It is difficult to match the colours today so the paws should be left as they are.

damage it will do him may be irreparable and he will hate the whole experience. Before cleaning you must make sure that his fabric is strong enough to withstand the process – if it is very fragile then seek expert advice. It is better to use a liquid detergent that is for delicates and wool rather than washing-up liquid or shampoo, which can create too much lather. Put ½ litre (1 pint) of warm water in a bowl and add a dessertspoon of the detergent. Whisk it until it foams and then apply the foam with a baby sponge to the bear, using a circular motion. Do not scrub. Remove the foam immediately and, using a clean cloth wrung out in warm water, wipe the bear gently. You will find that the dirt falls away. Keep repeating this until all the soap is removed. On the final rinse, put a dessertspoon of good-quality fabric conditioner in the water. This will leave his coat soft and silky. Remember that at all times you should avoid making him too wet, as this is just a surface wash. You can then pat him dry with a towel and, if possible, put him in an airing cupboard for two to three days. Alternatively, you can use a hairdryer on a very low setting held 15cm (6in) away from him. When he is dry, fluff up his fur with a soft brush.

MANICURE AND PEDICURE

Teddies' paws and feet are important identification aids. The style of claw stitching and paw covering is individual to each maker and often a label will still be attached to one foot. It is always best to leave the original pads in place, even if there are holes. You can patch them, but if a hole is too big and the stuffing is falling out then the pad will

before he is introduced to your hug, otherwise the infestation will spread to your other bears as well as to the carpets and furnishings. My preferred method is to take a black dustbin liner, place the bear in it and gather the top together, leaving a small hole. Then spray inside with a proprietary brand of moth repellent, making sure that you do this in a well-ventilated area. You should not spray directly onto the bear itself and it is best to seal the bag up afterwards and leave it for up to two weeks in order to allow time for any eggs to hatch so that the creatures that emerge will also be killed. Another method, which some people prefer, is to seal your bear in a polythene bag and place him in the freezer. I find this method rather extreme and it does not always kill all the bugs. After a period of isolation, you should then remove the bear from the bag and brush him with a soft brush to remove loose dust and dirt and moth husks.

BATH TIME

The method I am describing here applies just to mohair bears (for other fabrics there may be better alternatives) and need be done only if your new bear is very dirty. Teddies need to be clean but never put a bear in a washing machine or send him to the dry cleaners. The

CHANGING APPEARANCES
This early Steiff bear is very fragile so his sailor jacket actually protects him from suffering from further damage. He was in fact restored

many years ago. During this time a hole in the top of his muzzle was darned, which gathered the fabric together and gave his face a new, rather pointed look.

CARE & RESTORATION

have to be re-covered. If you do this you should still leave the remains of the original pad underneath. Try and get hold of felt to match the original – German wool felt is suitable for old bears and is obtainable from specialist suppliers. Acrylic felt is also available in many shades but is not always suitable for early bears. Some bears have cardboard inserts in their feet – try and leave the original in place but if it is damaged then replace it using flat cardboard cut to shape. Claw stitching can easily be replaced, often by following the original marks. Simple repairs such as these are possible but if you are in any doubt about what to do then ask an expert to do it for you rather than carrying out the work yourself.

STUFFING

Over the years the stuffing in old bears can become saggy and may even disintegrate. In such cases, restuffing a bear can help to conserve him. Restuffing can also make your bear look young again, although it is better to leave him with a slight droop of the head as this will add to his charm. Most old bears are stuffed with a mixture of kapok and wood wool, which is available from specialist suppliers.

However, during and after World War II a cotton waste product called sub-stuffing was used. This was sometimes mixed with kapok and in the 1950s and '60s bears were stuffed with foam chippings. The latter can sometimes disintegrate to a sticky dust. There is only one remedy for this and that is to empty the bear and restuff it with polyester stuffing. This stuffing is inexpensive and is an easy material to work with. It is obtainable from craft shops and is also suitable for many types of bears.

Most old bears have their final handsewn seam located at the back and their arms and legs have their seams positioned at the top, near the joints. Each of these can be unpicked very carefully so that you can restuff your bear yourself. It is definitely worth the effort as, when your bear has been restuffed, I assure you that you will be pleased to see him sitting up straight again and looking so much happier to be back to his old self.

RESTORING FRAGILE BEARS

Even though this fragile bear is not very old, the fabric was thin and had a large hole in it. In such cases it is better to line the hole with some matching mohair and then to sew very carefully around the edge to secure the repair.

BEFORE AND AFTER
These pictures show what this bear, c.1970, looked like before (left) and after (right) restoration work had been done. The bear was fragile and the owner did not want his facial features restored in case it changed his character. So he was just cleaned, repaired and new stuffing was added in his arms.

REPLACING LIMBS
This rare, red Farnell bear had lost his right arm. In order for a new arm to be made, mohair had to be dyed to match the colour as closely as possible. Then the arm was created by copying the pattern of the existing arm. This work naturally demands a very high level of restoration skill.

COSMETIC SURGERY

Your bear's face will be very special to you, particularly if he was your childhood friend and you now associate the battered nose and odd eyes with fond memories. So, before you restore him, think carefully about how you want him to look, as it is a matter of personal choice. Remember that if you make too many changes he will no longer be the bear that you know and love as his character will have changed significantly. If you decide to send him to an expert for repair, it is also important to let them know which features you would like to be left untouched and which you are happy for them to restore.

However, there are some things that should be attended to and can be changed without altering the character, as long as you stick to using the correct materials. A missing ear can easily be dealt with by unpicking the seam of the remaining one, dividing it into two and adding more fabric to the back of each one. When replacing eyes, you can purchase glass eyes on wires from specialist suppliers. Just ensure that you get the right size otherwise your bear could look very strange. Noses have often suffered from hundreds of kisses and therefore need restitching. Do make sure that you stitch the nose following the original design otherwise you will change the bear's character too much. And don't forget his smile – look for the marks where the stitching used to be and follow those.

Hair loss can be a particular problem with old bears if they have been handled a lot. There is no cure for baldness but thinning of the hair can be improved: you will find that when your bear is clean and fluffed up, the coat will look much thicker. Holes in the fabric can also be dealt with. Cover over holes with a patch that has been matched to the original fabric as closely as possible. This will stop the stuffing from spilling out.

If you feel that you can tackle the job of replacing a joint, then safety joints made from plastic are available from craft shops and are suitable for newer bears. Older bears need cardboard joints with metal cotter pins, which are available from specialist suppliers. Squeakers and growlers have often stopped working and sometimes it is possible to repair them but this is a lengthy process. They are available from specialist suppliers but it may be best just to leave the original one in the bear, as long as you make sure that it is not pressing on the fabric too much.

MAINTENANCE

Once bears have been cleaned and restored they only need a little regular maintenance. Keeping them free of dust is a priority, so a regular grooming with a soft brush and an annual wipe-down with a damp cloth wrung out with warm water should be done. It is also a good idea to keep lavender bags and cedar blocks nearby to deter moths. Do not sit your bears in direct light, for example on a windowsill, as this will cause them to dry out, rot and fade.

All types of bears need a cool place to sit out of the sunlight. If you wish to store a bear, never ever put him in a polythene bag. Instead place him in a cardboard box and wrap him in acid-free tissue or an old cotton pillowslip, and store him in a dry, cool place.

Old bears must be handled gently. Their days of being children's playthings are over and they need a quiet retirement, so do treat them with the respect that they deserve.

LOSING HAIR
It is not just very old bears that suffer from hair loss as comparatively new bears can be affected by this problem too. This bear from c.1950 has lost a lot of his hair and so only the mohair backing is left intact. It is not possible for the hair to be replaced, and the cleaning of a bear in this sort of condition is best left to an expert.

DISPLAY & DRESSING BEARS

How you display your bears is really your own personal choice and will probably be governed by the amount of space available in your home as well as the size of your bears. You may decide to have some sitting on the settee in your living room or to put up shelves in a spare room for them. Whatever you do, be warned that bears have a habit of spreading out and you may soon find them all over your home! And whether or not you dress your bears is again totally up to you. Some people love the extra challenge of finding or making clothes for their bears, while others like to leave their bears exactly how they find them. Sometimes, though, dressing a bear is necessary for very practical reasons – for example, you may have to dress a fragile bear just to hold him together. And of course some bears come already dressed; if the bear is of a ripe old age, these vintage clothes can tell a story all of their own.

DISPLAYING YOUR BEARS

There are various things to consider when you first come to decide how to display your bears. For example, if you just have one solitary bear, it is often a good idea to display him sitting in his own chair. If you have quite a few bears, though, it is nice to display them in a group. Size is obviously a consideration as this will have an impact on where you can place your bears, but a larger bear grouped together with two smaller ones looks lovely, especially if they are of a similar age. The top of a chest of drawers in the bedroom can be a good place for bears, with the small bears sitting on the large bears' laps.

OUT OF HARM'S WAY

However you decide to display your bears, you must first make sure that they are out of the reach of children and animals. This is very important if you have a collection of older bears, as they will be quite fragile and will need to be left in peace. Even if you decide to keep

> **DISPLAYING MINIATURE BEARS**
> These miniature Steiff bears are all dressed in knitted and crocheted outfits. The dolls' house furniture is c.1910 and the ornaments and books make good additions to the arrangement. A display such as this really shows off the bears to advantage and would also look nice in a glass cabinet.

LOOKING AFTER CLOTHES

If you are lucky enough to have a bear wearing vintage clothing and feel the clothes could be safely washed, then always use a handwash liquid detergent and cool water. You should also always dry the clothes flat. Your bear and its clothing, whether new or vintage, need to be kept dust-free. If your bears are not kept behind protective glass then move them regularly and gently brush the clothes – you will be surprised how much dust collects in the folds of the fabric.

FINDING ACCESSORIES

You may also like to dress up your bears using various types of accessories along with, or instead of, clothing. It can be a lot of fun to find accessories to go with bears, although it can also be quite time-consuming. Boot fairs, flea markets and antique fairs are among the many places to look and again the list is endless as to what will work well. Rattles do look particularly nice hung on a piece of ribbon around a bear's neck. The price that you pay for such accessories can vary greatly. For example, an early silver antique baby's rattle can cost you several hundred pounds, but a plastic or celluloid one will cost you a lot less. Old pocket watches that don't work can be quite cheap and these can also be hung around a bear's neck. Old glasses sitting on a bear's nose can also look attractive. If your bear is wearing a baby gown then you can pick up old brooches to pin to the dress. Necklaces, badges and medals are popular items as well. If you have a larger girl bear, and can find a small basket to hang on her arm, it is fun to fill it with knick-knacks such as old sewing items, bits of antique lace and perhaps an old photograph. It is always worth experimenting to find unusual ways of dressing up your bears.

ACCESSORIES AND CLOTHES
This lovely Steiff bear, dated c.1908, is 42cm (28in) high and looks extremely handsome indeed in his sailor jacket. Sailor outfits were popular with children during this period so the bear has been dressed to reflect that fashion. He also has an interesting collection of brooches and badges pinned to his jacket, and even a necklace around his neck.

FAKES

- Many of the commonly found fakes have black button eyes and are made to look similar to early Steiff bears with very long arms and exaggerated humps. However, the fabric used is not mohair.

- Sometimes they are made in coloured fabric; even bright green bears have been found. They are often unnaturally dirty.

Collecting vintage teddy bears has been a popular pastime for many years, and as the demand for old bears has grown so unfortunately the supply has diminished. Prices have risen as reports appear in the press about record prices achieved for vintage bears at auction. The result is that unscrupulous individuals seek to capitalize on this situation by making fake bears that look deliberately old and dirty, as though they have been found in an attic, and with all the characteristics of an old bear. They then attempt to pass them off as genuine to unsuspecting general antique dealers and country auction houses, or direct to collectors. Soft toy teddy bears are not the only fakes, as carved wooden Black Forest bears from the smallest sizes right up to large umbrella stands are being imported from the Far East. These often turn up at flea markets and auctions and can fool the unsuspecting collector. It can be so disappointing when the bargain we think we've found turns out not to be what it seemed.

RECOGNIZING A FAKE

Familiarizing yourself with the characteristics of bears, especially the fabrics used, will help to guard against being taken in by a fake. The fabric is often the giveaway, as it is usually not mohair but a type of cotton velour and sometimes it can be really dirty in an attempt to make it look old. This dirt is almost impossible to remove as it is usually greasy – not like the dust that settles in mohair over the years. These fake bears may have features associated with vintage bears of various eras, resulting in a bear that looks all wrong, is often out of proportion and not like any bear you will find in this or any other teddy bear book.

Some bears are made in an attempt to imitate Steiff: the feet of these bears are very long, but not the right shape, and they sometimes have leather or cotton paw pads, which is also wrong as Steiff never used leather on its bears' paws. Even a centre seam may be added to make it look authentic, and long shaved muzzles and black button eyes are also common. Another type of fake to look out for is those bears with glass eyes (as opposed to the more modern plastic) and a bald patch on the tummy to deceive the buyer into thinking that is where a squeaker was pressed many times over the years. Usually made of cotton velour, the fabric is invariably distressed to make it look worn, and old knitted clothing may be added. This type of fake often turns up on bric-a-brac stalls at antique shows and flea markets, and most often the stall holder will believe that it came from an old lady who had it from childhood. However, general stall holders are unlikely to know much about bears, and if you do not get a receipt then there is little you can do if you find you have bought a fake.

Fakes can even turn up in auction houses with some regularity, and may be described in the catalogue giving details of age and possible maker. But auctioneers are not always experts on old bears and they too can be deceived; usually if a mistake is pointed out to them they will correct it before the auction goes ahead. Old bears also appear in Internet auctions, but again so do fakes, and it may be harder to spot them from a photograph than seeing them in person, so beware.

As well as making bears from scratch, some fraudsters will use existing bears, such as modern replicas made by Steiff, and alter them to look older by removing the new labels and buttons and dirtying the fur. As it is a replica the shape will be right, and these have been slipped into auctions and successfully passed off as vintage bears. Teddy bear artists often design their bears in the vintage style, and if these bears have all their labels removed and are dirtied up, they too can easily be taken for the real thing. Another way of faking is to have a small synthetic bear (usually made in the Far East) surrounded by antique miniature objects, such as pieces of lace, china, cotton reels and old photographs, often in a glass-fronted case to appear more authentic.

These are just some of the ways that bears are faked, so learning as much as possible about old bears is the best safeguard against fraud. Buying from a reputable source, where a proper headed receipt is given with a description and approximate date of the bear, will give you security and peace of mind. However, do not abandon boot fairs and flea markets altogether, as authentic bargains do still turn up.

TWO FAKE BEARS
These bears are typical of the traditional-style fakes that appear on the market.

GLOSSARY

All-in-one
A bear that has been made from one single piece of material.

Alpaca Plush
Very soft woolly plush made of yarn spun from the fleece of the alpaca llama.

Arctophile
A person who is passionate about bears and usually an avid collector.

Artist Bear
A bear that is handmade by an individual artist, sometimes made as one-of-a-kind, or as a limited-edition bear.

Art-silk Plush
A synthetic material, originally used in the manufacture of rayon stockings and first used on teddy bears in the late 1920s.

Bisque
A malleable unglazed ceramic material used to make dolls' heads.

Boot-button Eyes
The wooden eyes used on early bears, named after the black buttons on boots and shoes, that fasten with a metal hook.

Bound-stitched Nose
A wide rectangular-shaped nose, introduced in 1938, with vertical stitching topped by a single horizontal stitch.

Composition
A mixture of substances, including plaster of Paris, glue, cloth and wood, used to make dolls' heads and other toy parts.

Cotter Pin
A two-pronged metal pin that fastens the card disc joints of early bears.

Cotton Plush
A cheap quality plush used during and immediately after World War II when mohair was in short supply.

Distressed Plush
Mohair that has been treated to make it appear old – a technique that is popular among bear artists and manufacturers making replica bears.

Dual Plush
A two-tone plush, usually with one colour tipping the ends of the mohair, used most commonly in the 1920s.

Fairy Foam
All-in-one foam stuffing used in British bears of the 1960s.

Googly Eyes
Distinctively large bulbous eyes, often with sideways-glancing pupils.

Growler (Tilt Growler)
A voice box inside a bear that growls or roars when the bear is tipped.

Helvetic
The manufacturer of musical movements used inside bears – often mistaken as the manufacturer of the bears themselves.

Hug
A group or collection of teddy bears, usually displayed in a decorative and appealing way.

Inset Muzzle
A bear's nose made from separate material to the rest of the face, often in a contrasting colour or texture.

Kapok
A natural lightweight fibre made from the seed pod of a tropical tree, used for stuffing bears and often combined with wood wool.

Layaway Service
A service offered by many shops whereby the vendor will keep the bear for a mutually agreed period, once a deposit is paid, and the remainder of the cost can be paid in monthly instalments.

Locked-in Safety Eyes
A child-safe design comprising a plastic eye with an integral black bolt that forms the pupil, fastened to the bear by a washer.

Mohair Plush
Fabric made originally from the fleece of angora goats but now usually a combination of wool and cotton.

Muzzled Bear
A bear with a muzzle guard, first made by Steiff in 1908 and inspired by German performing bears that were popular at the time.

Replica Bear
A modern version of an antique bear, made by the same manufacturer often using the original pattern. Often a limited-edition bear.

Rexine
A leather cloth used mainly on the paw pads of English bears post World War II.

Rod Bear
A design of Steiff bear made in 1904–05 with metal rod jointing instead of card.

Sub-stuffing
Stuffing made from the waste of cotton manufacture, used during World War II when kapok was unavailable.

Ultrasuede
A US term for a synthetic fabric that resembles suede, used in the 1970s.

Webbed-claw Stitching
A distinctive style of stitching where the claws are joined together in a web pattern, as used by Merrythought for example.

Wood Wool (Excelsior)
Long fine wood shavings – traditional teddy bear stuffing, often combined with kapok.

Yorkshire Cloth
Mohair plush woven in Yorkshire, England, and used on British and German bears.

DIRECTORY

BEAR CUB RESCUED BY LIBEARTY
Libearty is a worldwide campaign for the welfare of bears, launched by WSPA in 1992, that aims to prevent acts of cruelty and exploitation by bringing them to the attention of millions of people.

CHARITABLE ORGANIZATIONS:

UK
Libearty
WSPA
(World Society for the Protection of Animals)
PL58
89 Albert Embankment
London SE1 7TP
Tel: (0044) 20 7793 0540
Fax: (0044) 20 7793 0208
www.wspa.org.uk

Paddington's Action Club
Vincent House
Horsham
West Sussex RH12 2DP
Tel: (0044) 1403 210406
Fax: (0044) 1403 210541
E-mail: info@actionresearch.co.uk
(the proceeds from membership fees help raise funds for medical research through Action Research)

USA
Good Bears of the World
PO Box 13097, Toledo
Ohio 43613
www.goodbearsoftheworld.org
(an international charity organization, run by volunteers, that gives teddy bears to those in crisis situations)

AUSTRALIA
Bears Who Care
c/o Sue Maynard
PO Box 6106
Karingal
Victoria 3199
Tel: (0061) 3 9770 2955
www.alphalink.com.au/~suevill/bwc1.html

CLUBS:

UK
Boating Bears
c/o Pam Chester-Browne
23 Eden Avenue
Culcheth
Warrington
Cheshire WA3 5HX
E-mail:
pam@chester-browne.freeserve.co.uk

Dean's Collectors Club
Pontnewynydd Industrial Estate
Pontypool
Gwent NP4 6YY
Tel: (0044) 1495 764881
Fax: (0044) 1495 764883
www.deansbears.com
(magazine, factory open-days, £25 UK, $50 USA, £35 rest of world)

Especially Bears Group
38 Falkland Road
Chandlers Ford
Eastleigh
Hampshire SO53 3GD
Tel: (0044) 23 8036 9391
Fax: (0044) 23 8061 3616

Hugglets Teddy Bear Club
PO Box 290, Brighton
East Sussex BN2 1DR
Tel: (0044) 1273 697974
Fax: (0044) 1273 626255
E-mail: info@hugglets.co.uk
www.hugglets.co.uk
(annual Teddy Bear Guide, entrance to all Hugglets festivals, £12 UK, £14 elsewhere)

Just Golly! Collectors Club
Mrs A.K. Morris
9 Wilmar Way
Seal, Sevenoaks
Kent TN15 0DN
Tel: (0044) 1732 762379
E-mail: quinntheeskimo@btinternet.com
www.gollycorner.co.uk

Lytham St Annes Doll & Teddy Club
Isobel Ridley
20 Cambridge Road
Lytham St Annes
Lancashire FY8 5PJ
Tel: (0044) 1253 736814

Merrythought International Collectors Club
Ironbridge
Telford
Shropshire TF8 7NJ
Tel: (0044) 1952 433116 (ext 21)
Fax: (0044) 1952 432054
E-mail: contact@merrythought.co.uk

Protectabear Club
Lower Eaves, Park Road
Chapel-en-Frith
High Park, Derbyshire SK23 9UA
Tel: (0044) 1298 816000
Fax: (0044) 1298 816222
www.protectabear.com

Robin Rive Collectors Club
c/o Countrylife New Zealand
Box 3604, Brentwood
Essex CM14 4RY
Tel: (0044) 1708 703650
E-mail: rrbears@robinrive.com
www.robinrive.com

Tedi Bach Hug
Pebby Morton
1 Blandford Road
Ipswich
Suffolk IP3 8SL
Tel: 01473 727440
E-mail: j.morton@virgin.net
(club for makers of miniature bears,
designers and collectors, newsletter,
kits and bear supplies)

USA
Capers 'n' Teddies International Club
c/o Melanie Troutman
4460 South Alton Street
Greenwood Village
Colorado 80111-1205
Tel: (001) 303 221 2217
Fax: (001) 303 804 5765
E-mail: CNTeddies@aol.com
www.capersnteddies.com

Herrington's Teddy Bear Club
150 McCormick Avenue
Costa Mesa, California 92626
Tel: (001) 714 540 6657
Fax: (001) 714 540 0411
E-mail: sales@herringtonco.com
www.teddybearclub.com

**Merrythought International
Collector's Club**
PO Box 577
Oakdale
California 95361

Muffy VanderBear Club
c/o North American Bear Co. Inc.
401 North Wabash, Suite 500
Chicago
Illinois 60611
www.muffy.com/vbclub.htm

Steiff Club
PO Box 460
Raynham Center
Massachusetts 02768-0460
Tel: (001) 800 830 0429
www.steiff-club.com

JAPAN
Japan Teddy Bear Association
Harry Uchida (Chief Manager)
201 Daikanyama Pacific Mansion 10–14
Sarugaku-cho
Shibuya, Tokyo 150-0033
Tel: (0081) 3 3770 8539
Fax: (0081) 3 3770 8456
www.jteddy.com/english.html
(bi-monthly magazine)

Japan Teddy Bear Fan Club
3 Yokoshiba Building 3Fl 12–19
Daikanyama-cho
Sibuya
Tokyo 150-0034
Tel: (0081) 3 3770 6311
www.teddybear.co.jp
(bi-monthly magazine, free admission
to shows in March & October)

GERMANY
Steiff Club
Margarete Steiff GmbH
PO Box 1560
D-89530 Giengen/Brenz
Fax: (0049) 7322 131476
www.steiff.de/en

Teddy-Hermann GmbH
PO Box 1207
D-96112 Hirschaid
Tel: (0049) 9543 84820
(two newsletters a year plus a free
teddy for new members)

CANADA
**Merrythought International
Collector's Club**
601 Tradewinds Drive
Suite 3
Ancaster
Ontario L9G 4V5
Tel: (001) 905 304 0192

**Teddy Bear Collectors
Association of Alberta**
PO Box 3056
Sherwood Park
Alberta T8A 2A6

Teddy Bear Tymes
PO Box 21036
St Catharines Road
Ontario
Canada L2M 7X2
E-mail: tbt@niagara.com

AUSTRALIA
Arctophiles
Helen Lovitt-Raison
7 Harrow Street
Maylands 6051
E-mail: cavebeary@bigpond.com

FRANCE
Les Amis de Gueules de Miel
43 rue Cavendish
75019 Paris
Tel: (0033) 1 42 00 64 27
E-mail: gdmiel@cheerful.com
www.perso.wanadoofr/amis.gueulde
miel/agdmiel/english/gdmiel10.html
(promotes use of teddy bears for therapy)

Teddy's Patch
Le Club des Amis de l'Ours
34 Rue Lieu de Sante
76000 Londinieres
Tel: (0033) 235 932 146

USEFUL INTERNET WEBSITES:

www.teddy-bear-uk.com

www.teddybearsearch.com

www.aussieteddies.homestead.com

www.bearworld.com/bearly_listings/

www.sue-pearson.co.uk

**Sue Pearson Antique Dolls
& Teddy Bears**
13½ Prince Albert Street
The Lanes
Brighton
East Sussex BN1 1HE
UK
Tel: (0044) 1273 329247
E-mail: enquire@sue-pearson.co.uk

DIRECTORY

MANUFACTURERS:

The Dean's Company (1903)
Pontypool
Gwent NP4 6YY
Wales UK
Tel: (0044) 1495 764881
Fax: (0044) 1495 764883
E-mail: teddies@deansbears.com
www.deansbears.com

Gund
1 Runyons Lane
Edison
New Jersey 08817 USA
E-mail: askgund@gund.com
www.gund.com

Merrythought Ltd
Ironbridge
Telford
Shropshire TF8 7NJ
UK
Tel: (0044) 1952 433116
Fax: (0044) 1952 432054
Email: contact@merrythought.co.uk
www.merrythought.co.uk

North American Bear Co., Inc
401 N. Wabash
Suite 500
Chicago
Illinois 60611 USA
Tel: (001) 312 329 0020
Fax: (001) 312 329 1417

North American Bear Co., Inc
52 Morley Road
Tonbridge
Kent TN9 1RA
UK
Tel: (0044) 1732 360117
Fax: (0044) 1732 770124
E-mail: frepoint@cs.com
www.nabear.com

Russ Berrie and Co., Inc
111 Bauer Drive
Oakland
New Jersey 07436
USA
Tel: (001) 201 337 9000
E-mail: custserv@russberrie.com
www.russberrie.com

Russ Berrie (UK) Ltd
40 Oriana Way
Nursling Industrial Estate
Southampton
Hants SO16 OYU
UK
Tel: (0044) 1703 747747
Fax: (0044) 1703 747748

Steiff
PO Box 1560
D-89530 Giengen (Brenz)
Germany
Tel: (0049) 7322 1311
Fax: (0049) 7322 131 266
www.steiff.com

Clemens Spieltiere
Hans Clemens GmbH
Postfach 1161
D-74910 Kirchardt
Germany
E-mail: infor@clemens.de
www.clemens.de

Hermann Teddy Original
Teddy-Hermann GmbH
Postfach 1207
D-96114 Hirschaid
Germany
Tel: (0049) 9543 9161
Fax: (0049) 9543 9163
www.teddy-hermann.de

AUCTION HOUSES:

Bonhams
65–69 Lots Road
London SW10 0RN
UK
Tel: (0044) 20 7393 3951
Fax: (0044) 20 7393 3906
E-mail: toys@bonhams.com
www.bonhams.com

Christie's South Kensington
85 Old Brompton Road
London SW7 3LD UK
Tel: (0044) 20 7321 3335
Fax: (0044) 20 7321 3321
(two sales per year, in May and
December, devoted to teddy bears)

eBay On-line Auctions
www.ebay.com

Phillips Knowle
The Old House
Station Road
Knowle
Solihull
West Midlands B93 0HT UK
Tel: (044) 1564 776151
Fax: (0044) 1564 778069
E-mail: philknowl@hotmail.com
www.phillips-auctions.com

Theriault's
PO Box 151
Annapolis
Maryland 21404 USA
Tel: (001) 800 638 0422
Fax: (001) 410 224 2515
www.theriaults.com

Peddle DotNet
www.peddle.net

MUSEUMS:

UK
Alice's Wonderland
Brougham Hall
Penrith
Cumbria CA10 2DE
Tel: (0044) 1768 895648

The Bear Museum
38 Dragon Street
Petersfield
Hampshire GU31 4JJ
Tel: (0044) 1730 265108
E-mail: judy@bearmuseum.freeserve.co.uk
www.bearmuseum.co.uk

The British Bear Collection
Banwell Castle
Banwell
Somerset BS29 6NX
Tel: (0044) 1934 822263

**Bethnal Green Museum
of Childhood**
Cambridge Heath Road
London E2 9PA
Tel: (0044) 20 8980 2415
www.kidsnet.co.uk/museums/
bethgree.html

Broadway Dolls & Bears Museum
76 High Street
Broadway
Worcestershire WR12 7AJ
Tel: (0044) 1386 858323
E-mail: bearsanddolls@hotmail.com
www.jks.org/broadwaybearsanddolls.
html

The Dorset Teddy Bear Museum
Teddy Bear House
Antelope Walk
Dorchester
Dorset DT1 1BE
Tel: (0044) 1305 263200
Fax: (0044) 1305 268885
E-mail: info@teddybearhouse.co.uk
www.teddybearhouse.co.uk
www.teddybearmuseum.co.uk

Hamilton Toy Collection
111 Main Street
Callander
Perthshire FK17 8BQ
Tel: (0044) 18773 30004

**Ironbridge Gorge Museum
& Teddy Bear Shop**
Ironbridge
Telford
Shropshire TF8 7NJ
Tel: (0044) 1952 433029
E-mail: teddybears@ironbridge.org.uk
(The museum and shop focus on
Merrythought bears only, both new
and vintage bears)

Museum of Childhood
42 High Street
Edinburgh EH1 1TG
Tel: (0044) 131 529 4142
Fax: (0044) 131 558 3103

Park House
Park Street
Stow-on-the-Wold
Gloucestershire GL54 1AQ
Tel: (0044) 1451 830159
Fax: (0044) 1451 870809

Pollock's Toy Museum
1 Scala Street
London W1T 2HL
Tel: (0044) 20 7636 3452
E-mail: toytheatres@hotmail.com
E-mail: pollocks@tao2000.net

The Teddy Bear Museum
19 Greenhill Street
Stratford-upon-Avon
Warwickshire CV37 6LF
Tel: (0044) 1789 293160
www.teddybearmuseum.uk.com

**The Toy and
Teddy Bear Museum**
373 Clifton Drive North
Lytham St Annes
Lancashire FY8 2PA
Tel: (0044) 1253 713705

USA
The Teddy Bear Castle Museum
203 South Pine
Nevada City
California 95959

For information write to:
Ted d'Bear
PO Box 328
Nevada City
California 95959
Tel: (001) 530 265 5804
Fax: (001) 530 478 0728
E-mail: bearcastle@yahoo.com
www.teddybearcastle.com

Teddy Bear Museum of Naples
2511 Pine Ridge Road
Naples
Florida 34109
USA
Tel: (001) 941 598 2711
E-mail: info@teddymuseum.com
www.teddymuseum.com

IRELAND
Ted's Eclectic Lot
Haggard Street
Trim
County Meath
Ireland
Tel: (00353) 46 38350/36263
www.tedseclecticlot.ie

GERMANY
Margarete Steiff Museum
PO Box 1560
D-74910 Giengen (Brenz)
Germany
Tel: (0049) 7322 1311
www.steiff.com/the_museum.htm

SWITZERLAND
Puppenhausmuseum Basel
Steineck-Stiftung
Steinenvorstadt 1
CH-4051 Basel
Tel: (0041) 61 225 95 95
Fax: (0041) 61 225 95 96
www.puppenhausmuseum.ch

JAPAN
Teddy Bear Art Museum
"Michi & Hiro Takahashi's World"
11–17 Toyokawa-cho
Haksdate
Hokkaido 040-8430
Tel: (0081) 138 277070

Teddy Bear Museum
413-0232
Ito Shi
1041-56 Izukogen
Tel: (0081) 557 544485
Fax: (0081) 557 533190

DIRECTORY

BEAR ARTISTS:

UK

Christine Pike Bears
9 New Road
Lake
Nr Sandown
Isle of Wight PO36 9JN
Tel/Fax: (0044) 1983 403224
E-mail: PikeLewis@aol.com
www.christinepike.com

Companion Bears
6 Claremont Drive
Timperley
Altrincham
Cheshire WA14 5ND
Tel: (0044) 161 976 1877
Fax: (0044) 161 969 1505
E-mail: combears@libertysurf.co.uk

Fluff and Stuff by Kay Turmeau
6 Hawkes Close
Wokingham
Berkshire RG41 2SZ
Tel: (0044) 118 978 6267

Jo Greeno
E-mail: jo.greeno@freezone.co.uk

Minikins by Maggie Spackman
51 Fotherley Road
Mill End, Rickmansworth
Hertfordshire WD3 8QQ
Tel: (0044) 1923 447147
E-mail:
minikins@maggiesminikins.fsnet.co.uk
www.maggiesminikins.fsnet.co.uk

Norbeary Bears
14 Claymere Avenue
Norden
Rochdale
Lancashire OL11 5WB
Tel/Fax: (0044) 1706 659819
E-mail: norbeary@btinternet.com

Portobello Bear Company
The Studio
Lower Ground Floor

37 Queen Street
Scarborough
North Yorkshire YO11 1HQ
Tel: (0044) 1723 377475
Fax: (0044) 1723 374685
E-mail: portobellobearco@compuserve.com
www.portobellobearco.com

Sally Lambert
Bowfield Cottage
North Lane
West Hoathly
Sussex RH19 4QF

Shoebutton Bears
11 Southern Road
Sale
Cheshire M33 6HP
Tel: (0044) 161 282 8636
E-mail: sue_wilkes@hotmail.com
www.shoebuttonbears.co.uk

Somethings Bruin
Jill Baxter
Greenacre
Dill Road
Milton
Tenby
Pembrokeshire SA70 8PR
Tel: (0044) 1646 651361
E-mail: somethingsbruin@beeb.net
www.somethingsbruin.com

USA
Joan Woessner
Bear Elegance Exclusives
31759 Corte Rosario
Temecula
California 92592
Tel: (001) 909 587 2775
Fax: (001) 909 587 6165
E-mail: woes44@earthlink.net

IRELAND
Ballythread Bear
Leila Stewart
Caher
Ballinrobe
Co. Mayo
Tel/Fax: (00353) 92 41 851

AUSTRALIA
StrawBearies
PO Box 34
Anglesea
3230 Victoria
Tel: (0061) 3 5263 2773
Fax: (0061) 3 5263 2773

GERMANY
Original Rica-Bär
Ulrike and Claude Charles
Friesenstrasse 5
32760 Detmold
Tel: (0049) 5231 59750
Fax: (0049) 5231 580018
E-mail: mail@rica-baer.de
www.rica-baer.de

JAPAN
Fairy Chuckle
Hiro and Michi Takahashi
c/o Aobadai P.O.
Yokohama 227-8799
Tel: (0081) 90 2942 3574

SOUTH AFRICA
Changle Bears
71 Vincent Gardens North
Vincent
East London 5247
Tel: (0027) 43 7269331
Fax: (0027) 43 7431130
E-mail: footman@intekom.co.za
www.changlebears.co.za

SUPPLIERS OF BEARMAKING MATERIALS & KITS:

UK
Admiral Bears Supplies
37 Warren Drive
Ruislip
Middlesex
HA4 9RD
Tel: (0044) 20 8868 9598
E-mail: info@admiral-bears.com
www.admiral-bears.com

Bridon Bears
Bears Cottage
42 St Michael's Lane
Bridport
Dorset DT6 3RD
Tel: (0044) 1308 420796

Bear Bits
The Florins
Silver Street
Minting
Horncastle
Lincolnshire LN9 5RP
Tel: (0044) 1507 578360
E-mail: ashburner@bearbits.com
www.bearbits.com

Christie Bears Supplies
Dept MG
Solva House
Brawdy Business Park
Brawdy
Haverfordwest
Pembrokeshire SA62 6NP
Tel: (0044) 800 074 2327
E-mail: christiebs@aol.com
www.christiebears.co.uk

Emmary Bears
Ridgeway
Bodmin Hill, Lostwithiel
Cornwall PL22 0AJ
Tel: (0044) 1208 872251
www.emmarybears.co.uk

The Glass Eye Co
School Bank Road
Llanrwst
Gwynedd LL26 0HU
Tel: (0044) 1492 642220
Fax: (0044) 1492 641643
E-mail: STS.northwales@virgin.net
www.glasseyes.com

Growlies
15 Thorn Brae
Johnstone
Strathclyde PA5 8HF
Tel: (0044) 1505 336551
E-mail: teddies@growlies.co.uk

Lyrical Bears
PO Box 111
Welwyn Garden City
Hertfordshire AL6 0XT
Tel: (0044) 1438 351651
E-mail: info@lyrical-bears.co.uk
www.lyrical-bears.co.uk

Norbeary Fabrics
14 Claymere Avenue
Norden
Rochdale
Lancashire OL11 5WB
Tel: (0044) 1706 659819
E-mail: norbeary@btinternet.com

Ted's Place Too
Blakemere Craft Centre
Chester Road
Sandiway
Cheshire CW8 2EB
Tel: (0044) 1606 888814
E-mail: Tedsplace@btinternet.com

Teddy Bear Warehouse Ltd
Unit 11
D2 Trading Estate
Castle Road
Sittingbourne
Kent ME10 3RH
Tel: (0044) 1795 478775
Fax: (0044) 1795 474494

USA
Edinburgh Imports Inc
1121 Lawrence Drive
Newbury Park
California 91320
Tel: (001) 805 376 1700
Fax: (001) 805 376 1711
www.edinburgh.com

Haida Supplies
29533 Canvasback Drive
Easton
Maryland 21601
Tel: (001) 410 770 5100
www.haidasup.com

Spare Bear Parts
792 East Highway 66
Tijeras
New Mexico 87059
Tel: (001) 505 286 5005
Fax: (001) 505 286 5018
www.sparebear.com

CANADA
Dear Bears MarketPlace
4747 Quebec Street
Vancouver
British Columbia V5V 3M2
Tel: (001) 604 872 2508
Fax: (001) 604 872 2504
www.dear-bears.com

Disco Joints & Teddies
2 Ridgewood Place, Box 468
St Clements
Ontario N0B 2MO
Tel: (001) 519 699 5762
Fax: (001) 519 699 4525
www.discojoints.on.ca

AUSTRALIA
Cobwebs & Pussycats
PO Box 1,000
Coffs Harbour
New South Wales 2450
Tel: (0061) 2 6651 1877
www.midcoast.com.au/~pussycat

FRANCE
Arts et Creations
83 Rue Médéric
92250 La Garenne Colombes
Tel: (0033) 1 47 60 15 58
Fax: (0033) 1 47 89 50 23
www.artsetcreations.com

NETHERLANDS
Berelijn
Voorstraat 269
3311 EP, Dordrecht
Tel: (0031) 78 631 8028
Fax: (0031) 78 631 0498
E-mail: berelijn@wxs.nl
www.berelijn.com

CALENDAR OF EVENTS

Please contact the organizers of each fair before travelling, to confirm date and venue.

JANUARY

IDEX
Civic Auditorium, San Francisco, California USA. Tel: Idex (001) 404 378 2217

Linda's Teddy Bear, Doll & Antique Toy Show & Sale
Scottish Rite Center, San Diego, California USA. Tel: Linda Mullins (001) 760 434 7444

Raggedy Ann Doll and Teddy Bear Convention
The Bahia Shrine Auditorium, Orlando, Florida USA. E-mail: raggedyman@aol.com

Teddy Bear Spring Training
264 N Center Street, Mesa, Arizona USA. Tel: ABC Productions (001) 815 464 3470

FEBRUARY

Bankstown Doll & Bear Fair
Bankstown Town Hall, Bankstown Australia. Tel: Bear Facts (0061) 2 4868 1338

The London International Antique & Artist Dolls, Toys, Miniatures & Teddy Bear Fair
Kensington Town Hall, London UK. Tel: Granny's Goodies (0044) 20 8693 5432

Teddies & Friends
The Red Lion Hotel, Seattle, Washington USA. Tel: Pat Moore Productions (001) 503 775 3324

Teddy Bear Fair
Holiday Inn Bell Tower, Fort Myers, Florida USA. Tel: Bright Star Promotions (001) 502 423 7827

Winter Bearfest
Kensington Town Hall, London UK. Tel: Hugglets (0044) 1273 697974

MARCH

Annual Teddy Bear Affair
Nights of Columbus Hall, Syracuse, New York USA. Tel: Dianne Liddic (001) 315 475 9931

Doll and Teddy Fair
The National Motorcycle Museum, Bickenhill, Nr Birmingham UK. Tel: Doll and Teddy Fairs (0044) 1530 274377

Essex Teddybear Fair
Forte Posthouse, Brentwood, Essex UK. Tel: Teddybear Traders (0044) 1702 585692

Japan Teddy Bear Festival
Ebisu Garden Place "Garden Hall", Tokyo Japan. Tel: Japan Teddy Bear Fan Club (0081) 3 3770 6311

Leeds Doll and Teddy Fair
Pudsey Civic Hall, Leeds UK. Tel: Dolly Domain Fairs (0044) 191 424 0400

APRIL

Annual International Teddy Bear Convention
Miners Foundry, Nevada City, California USA. Tel: Teddy Bear Castle (001) 530 265 5804

Bears and Dolls
NEC (National Exhibition Centre) Birmingham UK. Tel: (0044) 121 749 7330

The Midlands Teddy Bear Festival
Telford Moat House, Telford, Shropshire UK. Tel: Midlands Teddy Bear Festivals (0044) 1952 433924

Rochester Teddy Bear Fair
Corn Exchange, Rochester, Kent UK. Tel: Rochester Teddy Bear Fairs (0044) 1634 234378

MAY

Border Bear Fair
The Wynd Theatre, Melrose, Scotland UK. Tel: Border Bear Fairs (0044) 1896 823854

Buitenwerwagting Teddy Fair
Constantia, Cape Town, South Africa. Tel: Sanette Gibson (0027) 8 288 1403

The Hug-In
Ramada Hotel, Toronto, Ontario Canada. Fax: Vicki McAllister (001) 905 668 7879

The Midlands Teddy Bear Event
NAC Stoneleigh Park, Coventry, UK. Tel: EMF Publishing (0044) 1903 244900

Southern Highlands Doll & Bear Fair
Bowral, New South Wales Australia. Tel: Bear Facts (0061) 2 4868 1338

Spring Bearfest
Kensington Town Hall, London UK. Tel: Hugglets (0044) 1273 697974

Tyneside Doll and Teddy Fair
Newcastle Racecourse, Newcastle UK. Tel: Dolly Domain Fairs (0044) 191 424 0400

JUNE

Hugbeary Den Winter Fair
Hillcrest Scout Hall, Hillcrest, Natal South Africa. Tel: Lynda Cansfield (0027) 31 765 2426

Japan Teddy Bear Convention
Tokyo Trade Centre, Tokyo Japan. Fax: Japan Teddy Bear Association (0081) 3 3770 8456 or (001) 719 266 9564 in USA

The London International Antique & Artist Dolls, Toys, Miniatures & Teddy Bear Fair
Kensington Town Hall, London UK. Tel: Granny's Goodies (0044) 20 8693 5432

Premier Bear Affair
Sydney Town Hall, Sydney Australia.
Tel: Bear Facts (0061) 2 4868 1338

Steiff Festival
Town Hall, Giengen, Germany. Tel: GAF
Günther Pfeiffer (0049) 6128 970927

Teddy Bear Collection Show
Lyons-la-Foret, France. Tel: Le Club des
Amis de l'Ours (0033) 2 35 88 96 00

Teddy Bear Show
Salon Gueles de Miel, Paris France.
Tel: Les Amis de Gueles de Miel (0033)
1 42 00 64 27

Winter Wonderland Doll & Bear Fair
Brisbane, Queensland Australia.
Tel: Elizabeth (0061) 7 32 66 4529

JULY

**Annual Ann Arbor Original
Teddy Bear Show**
Weber's Inn, Ann Arbor, Michigan USA.
Tel: Bright Star Promotions (001) 502
423 7827

Annual Teddy Bear Jubilee
Doubletree Hotel, Overland Park, Kansas
USA. Tel: DBFH Studios (001) 913 485 9087

Kloof Doll and Teddy Fair
Durban, South Africa. Tel: Lynda Cansfield
(0027) 31 765 2426

AUGUST

Border Bear Fair
The Wynd Theatre, Melrose, Scotland UK.
Tel: Border Bear Fairs (0044) 1896 823854

**Linda's Teddy Bear, Doll &
Antique Toy Show & Sale**
San Diego, California USA. Tel: Linda
Mullins (001) 760 434 7444

Rocky Mountain Teddies
Holiday Inn, Colorado Springs, Colorado USA.
Tel: Pat Moore Prod. (001) 503 775 3324

Sigriswil Teddy Bear Festival
Sigriswil, Switzerland. Contact Marianne
Schmid on e-mail: tourcom@bluewin.ch

Teddies
Kensington Town Hall, London UK.
Tel: Hugglets (0044) 1273 697974

SEPTEMBER

Doll and Teddy Fair
The National Motorcycle Museum,
Bickenhill, Nr Birmingham UK. Tel: Doll
and Teddy Fairs (0044) 1530 274377

Essex Teddybear Fair
Forte Posthouse, Brentwood, Essex UK. Tel:
Teddybear Traders (0044) 1702 585692

**The London International Antique
& Artist Dolls, Toys, Miniatures
& Teddy Bear Fair**
Kensington Town Hall, Hornton Street,
London UK. Tel: Granny's Goodies (0044)
20 8693 5432

Spring Bear Fair
Berario, Johannesburg South Africa.
Tel: Nerina Roberts (0027) 11 678 5834

Sydney Bear Fair
Sydney, Australia. Tel: Brown Bear
Productions Pty Ltd (0061) 8 9272 4965

OCTOBER

The Event
Alexandra Palace, London UK. Tel: EMF
Publishing (0044) 1903 244900

Japan Teddy Bear Festival
Umeda Crystal Hall, Osaka Japan. Tel: Japan
Teddy Bear Fan Club (0081) 3 3770 6311

Leeds Doll and Teddy Fair
Pudsey Civic Hall, Leeds UK. Tel: Dolly
Domain Fairs (0044) 191 424 0400

The Midlands Teddy Bear Festival
Telford Moat House, Telford, Shropshire
UK. Tel: Midlands Teddy Bear Festivals
(0044) 1952 433924

Octobear Faire
Marriot Hotel, Schaumburg, Illinois USA.
Tel: ABC Productions (001) 815 464 3470

October Doll & Bear Extravaganza
Bowral, New South Wales Australia.
Tel: Bear Facts (0061) 2 4868 1338

Teddy Bear Fair
Stellenbosch, Cape Town, South Africa.
Tel: Brian Bredenkamp (0027) 21 887
9001

NOVEMBER

Bears and Dolls
NEC (National Exhibition Centre)
Birmingham UK. Tel: (0044) 121
749 7330

Teddy Bear Celebration
Kensington Town Hall, London UK.
Tel: Hugglets (0044) 1273 697974

DECEMBER

British Bear Fair
Hove Town Hall, Nr Brighton, Sussex UK.
Tel: British Bear Fair (0044) 1403 711511

Danville Annual Teddy Fair
Durban, South Africa. Tel: Lynda Cansfield
(0027) 31 765 2426

Teddy Bear Fair
Riverside Leisure Centre, Chelmsford,
Essex UK. Tel: Totally Teddies (0044)
1279 871110

FURTHER READING

When starting a collection it is a good idea to look at the many excellent books and magazines on teddy bears that are available, in order to read and learn about all the different types of bears and help you to recognize the makers and age of vintage bears. Books on bears can be found in the library, at bookshops or on the internet. If you want to collect new bears then many of the bear artists feature in specialist bear magazines, which are available at most newsagents.

BOOKS

Axe, John,
The Magic of Merrythought
(Hobby House Press, USA, 1986)

Beckett, Alison & Campione, Bunny,
Miller's Collecting Teddy Bears & Dolls:
The Facts at Your Fingertips
(Octopus Publishing Group Ltd, UK, 1996)

Brown, Michèle & Buntrock, Gerrit,
The Teddy Bear Hall of Fame: A Century
of Historic Bears Presented by the
Teddy Bear Museum
(Headline Book Publishing, UK, 1996)

Bull, Peter,
The Teddy Bear Book
(Hobby House Press, USA, 1983)

Cieslik, Jürgen & Marianne,
Teddy Bear Encyclopaedia
(Golden Horse Publishing, USA, 1998)

Cieslik, Jürgen & Marianne,
Button in the Ear Book
(Marianne Cieslik Verlag, Germany, 1989)

Cockrill, Pauline,
The Teddy Bear Encyclopedia
(Dorling Kindersley, UK, 1993)

Consalvi, Peter,
Collector Steiff Values
(Hobby House Press, USA, 1994 & 1996)

Fox Mandel, Margaret, *Teddy Bears &*
Steiff Animals (Collector Books, 1994)

Hockenberry, Dee, *More Enchanting*
Friends (Schiffer Publishing, USA, 1998)

Hockenberry, Dee,
Steiff Bears & Other Playthings
(Schiffer Publishing, USA, 2000)

Hugglets,
The UK Teddy Bear Guide 2002
(Hugglets Publishing, UK, 2001) – an
annual guide to all things bear-related

King, Constance Eileen,
The Century of the Teddy Bear
(Antiques Collectors' Club, UK, 1997)

Laing, Jennifer, *Teddy Bear Art: How*
to Design & Make Great Teddy Bears
(Hobby House Press, USA, 1998)

Manolis, Argie,
The Teddy Bear Sourcebook for
Collectors and Artists
(Betterway Books, 1996)

Merrett, Alicia,
The Complete Book of Teddy-Bear
Making Techniques
(Running Press Book Publishers, USA, 1998)

Mullins, Linda, *Teddy Bear Encyclopedia*
(Hobby House Press, USA, 1995)

Mullins, Linda, *Teddy Bears & Friends*
(Hobby House Press, USA, 2000)

Mullins, Linda,
The Teddy Bear Men: Historical Guide for
Collectors (Hobby House Press, USA, 1987)

Mullins, Linda, *Teddy Bears Past &*
Present, A Collector's Identification Guide
(Hobby House Press, USA, 1989)

Pearson, Sue, *Bears*
(De Agostini Editions Ltd., UK, 1995)

Pistorius Steiff, Rolf & Christel,
Sensational Teddy Bears
(Hobby House Press, USA, 1991)

Schoonmaker, Patricia W.,
A Collector's History of the Teddy Bear
(Hobby House Press, USA, 1981)

Upton, Rosalie,
The Secret Lives of Teddy Bears
(HarperCollins World, 1996)

Waring, Philippa & Peter,
Teddy Bears (Treasure Press, 1984)

Yenke, Ken, *Bing Bears & Toys*
(Schiffer Publishing, USA, 2000)

Yenke, Ken,
Teddy Bear Treasury:
Identification and Values
(Schroeder Publishing Inc., USA, 2000)

MAGAZINES

Bear Facts Review (M.A. Brooks,
Doll Digest Publishing, Australia)

Canadian Teddy Bear News (Patricia
Atchison, Atchison Literature Inc., Canada
www.teddybearnews.com)

Japan Teddy Bear Fan Club (Tokyo, Japan,
bi-monthly, free to members)

Teddy Bear Club International

Teddy Bear & Friends (Primedia
Publications, USA, published bi-monthly,
www.teddybearandfriends.com)

Teddy Bear Scene (EMF Publishing, UK)

Teddy Bear Times (UK publication,
www.teddybeartimes.com)

Teddy Bear Voice (Japan Teddy Bear
Association, Tokyo, Japan, bi-monthly,
free to members)

INDEX

ACKNOWLEDGMENTS

The author would like to thank her husband Michael for his hard work and patience and the following people for their help and contribution – Cathy and Chuck Steffes, Fiona Miller, Dottie Ayers, Pam Pudvine and Pat Rush. The publishers would like to thank those who provided images or items for photography.

OPG/Peter Anderson/Sue Pearson: front of jacket, p6, p11t, p38, p42t, p50cl, p52b, p53br, p92, p134; OPG/Michael Pearson/Fiona Miller: front flap, back of jacket, p5, p9, p84t, p85tl, p85bl, p87tl, p109tl, p112, p113 (all), p113b, p115tl, p115tr, p115cl, p115br, p126br, p137br, p140, p141t, p141b, p142; OPG/Michael Pearson/Sue Pearson: back flap, p7, p8, p10p11b, p12b, p12t, p13, p15, p17b, p19cr, p19bl, p21c, p22b, p23t, p23cr, p23b, p25t, p25c, p26, p27t, p27b, p29t, p29c, p31b, p32, p33t, p33c, p33b, p35t, p35c, p35b, p36, p37c, p39cr, p42b, p43t, p43b, p44bl, p44br, p45t, p45b, p47br, p49br, p50tl, p52tr, p57t, p59t, p59b, p61b, p64r, p65tl, p65c, p65bl, p65br, p70l, p71 tr, p71cl, p71br, p73tr, p75cl, p83br, p87br, p88bl, p90l, p107, p109tl, p109br, p111bl, p114t, p115bl, p119cl, p127cl, p127bl, p130r, p130b, p131tr, p133tl, p136t, p136b, p137tl, p139b, p143t, p144; Sue Pearson archive: full title, p24, p31c, p44c, p47 centre detail, p60, p61cl, p71tl, p79t, p79cl, p79cr, p80br, p118t, p118br, p129bl, p129br; OPG/Peter Anderson/Sue Pearson/Trevor Jacobs/Jenny Harrison: p14; OPG/Peter Anderson/Cathy & Chuck Steffes: p16, p17t, p17c, p18t, p18b, p19t, p19cl, p21b, p30lm p40, p51, p55t, p55c, p57cl, p57cr, p57b, p58t, p58b, p59c, p61t, p61cr, p67c, p69tl, p69br, p71bl, p76tl, p77t, p77bl, p83tl, p83bl, p86l, p86r, p87tr, p87bl, p88cr, p89tr, p89br, p108, p109bl, p110tl, p110cr, p110bl, p111tl, p111tr, p122 (all), p123 (all), p124 (all), p125 (all), p126 tl, p126bl, p127tl, p127tr, p127br, p128tl, p129c, p133tr, p133cr, p133bl; OPG/Michael Pearson/ Jenny Harrison: p20, p21t, p34t, p37cl, p41t, p41c, p62; OPG/Michael Pearson/Trevor Jacobs: p22t, p34b, p39t, p41b, p43c, p78 l, p78r, p80bl, p81tr, p81bl, p89cr, p116b, 118bl, p119tr; OPG/Michael Pearson/Pam Howells: p25b; OPG/Michael Pearson/Banwell Castle: p27c, p30r, p31t, p37t, p37b, p44t, p46, p47t, p47c, 47bl, p63t, p63cl, p63cr, p79b, p80t, p81tl, p81br, p89bl, p111br, p116t, p116 detail, p117 (all), p119cr, p119bl, p128bl, p128br, p129c, p130l, p131 tl, p131bl, p132 (all), p133br, p139t; Sue Pearson archive/Mike Crane: p28; OPG/Michael Pearson/Mike Crane: p29b; OPG/Peter Anderson/Trevor Jacobs/Janet Jacobs: p39bl, p39br; OPG/Peter Anderson/Trevor Jacobs: p48, p49t, p49bl, p50tr, p50br, p56t, p91cr; Dottie Ayers: p52tl, p53tl, p53tr, p53cl, p53cr, p53bl, p54t, p66l, p66 detail, p67t, p67b, p68br, p69tr, p69bl, p131bc, p131br; OPG/Michael Pearson/Stewart Sonne: p54b; Sue Pearson archive/Puppenhausmuseum, Basel: p55b, p56b, p64l, p64 bottom detail, p65tr, p66r, p67 details, p68tl, p70r, p70 bottom detail, p76 b, p77br, p91tr; OPG Kent/Childhood Memories, Farnham: p63b; OPG/Michael Pearson/Pam Pudvine: p72l, p73bl, p73br, p79br, p82, p82 detail, p89tl, p135, p143b; OPG/Private Collection: p72r, p73tl; OPG/Michael Pearson/Ted's Eclectic Lot: p74l, p74r, p74 details; OPG/Michael Pearson/Puppenhausmuseum, Basel: p75 tl, p75tr, p75bl, p75br; OPG/Michael Pearson/Sandra Wickenden: p83tr, p85tr, p85br, p87cl; OPG/Michael Pearson/Janet Jacobs: p84b, p88tl, p91tl, p91bl, p119tl; OPG/Peter Anderson/Janet Jacobs: p90r, p91br; OPG/Michael Pearson/Frank Webster: p93; OPG/Michael Pearson/Jo Greeno: p120 (all), p121 (all); OPG/Michael Pearson/Emily Anderson: p138bl; OPG/ Peter Anderson/Emily Anderson: p138t, p138br; Clemens Spieltiere GmbH, c/o AM International Agencies Ltd, 1 Granby Croft, Matlock Street, Bakewell, Derbyshire DE45 1ET, UK: p94t, p94b; The Dean's Rag Book Co Ltd, The Deans Company, Pontypool, Gwent NP4 6YY, UK: p95t, p95b; Gund UK Limited, Havelock House, Holme Road, Bamber Bridge, Preston. PR5 6BP, UK: p96t, p96c; Teddy-Hermann GmbH, Amlingstadter Str. 5, D-96114 Hirschaid, Germany: p96b, p97t; Merrythought Limited, Ironbridge, Telford, Shropshire. TF8 7NJ, UK: p97c, p97b; North American Bear Co, 52 Morley Road, Tonbridge, Kent TN9 1RA, UK: p98t, p98c; Russ Berrie (UK) Ltd, 40, Oriana Way, Nursling Industrial Estate, Southampton UK: p98b, p99t; Margarete Steiff GmbH, Postfach 1560, D-89530 Giengen/Brenz, Germany: p99c; Harrods, Knightsbridge, London UK: p99b; Sally Lambert: p100t; OPG/Michael Pearson/Portobello Bears: p100b; Shoebutton Bears: p101t; OPG/Michael Pearson/Strawbearies: p101c; OPG/Michael Pearson/Joan Woessner: p101b; Jo Greeno: p102t; OPG/Peter Anderson/Fluff and Stuff: p102c; Christine Pike Bears: p102b; Ballythread Bear: p103t; Original Rica-Bär: p103c; Minikins: p103b; Norbeary Bears: p104t; Somethings Bruin: p104c; Fairy Chuckle: p104b, p105t; Companion Bears: p105c; Changle Bears, South Africa: p105b; OPG/Peter Anderson/Sue Pearson/Trevor Jacobs/Janet Jacobs/Jenny Harrson: p106; WSPA, PL58, 89 Albert Embankment, London SE1 7TP, UK: p146